THE GREENBRIER RIVER TRAIL

THROUGH THE EYES OF HISTORY

D0752671

LIBRARY OF CONGRESS
CATALOG CARD NO. 96-69801

ISBN 1-57510-020-7

First Printing: March 1997
First Printing Revised Edition: July 2004

Typography and Composition: Arrow Graphics
Cover Design and Maps: Bill Vaughn

Photo Credits

COHS—Chesapeake and Ohio Historical Society
PCHS—Pocahontas County Historical Society

The cover photo shows the Chesapeake and Ohio Railway bridge
across the Greenbrier River at Watoga. The photograph © was taken
downstream from the bridge using an antique rotating panoramic
camera. The phtographer is Doug Chadwick, Hillsboro, W. Va. 24946.

PUBLISHED BY
Pictorial Histories Publishing Company, Inc.
1125 Central Avenue, Charleston, WV 25302
PHONE (304) 342-1848, FAX (304) 343-0594
wvbooks@verizon.net

Introduction

     *N*o doubt the users of the Greenbrier River Trail are aware of its original existence as a railroad. However, many of the people on the trail are of an age that has no personal knowledge of the importance railroads had in the life of the nation for the first half of this century. Other trail visitors are of an age that makes them well acquainted with railroads, but the physical evidence that exists today along the trail (particularly with leaves on the trees) gives little indication of what a busy stretch of railroad the Greenbrier Division of the Chesapeake and Ohio Railway was for many years. It is possible to pass the location of entire towns, some not so small, without having any idea that they once existed.

     A person spending a day trackside about 1910, for example, would have observed four passengers trains and several freight trains hauling out the production of about 25 sawmills, two tanneries, the area's farms, and smaller industries. The freights would also be bringing in the needs and wants, large and small, of the people of the Greenbrier Valley. Moving ahead to the mid 1920s, our observer would now find added to the schedule "timed" freight trains using the line as a route for traffic between Chicago and eastern cities. In both world wars, the Greenbrier line was one of the transportation corridors essential for victory. Those interested in such things would have observed over the years of steam power a large variety of engines on the Greenbrier trains, from small to large.

     Also, there is nothing about the Greenbrier River itself that gives evidence of its use for about 30 years as the way logs were moved to sawmills before the railroad was constructed. The annual late winter "log drive" on the river is an experience that is no longer possible to be described by someone who took part. Photographs can give us today only a partial idea of what it must have been like to handle logs in the high, cold water in the river.

No book is needed to enable the Greenbrier River Trail users to enjoy the beauty of the Greenbrier River Valley. It is the hope of the author of this book that knowing some of the pre-trail history will make your trip on the trail a more meaningful and enjoyable experience. Maybe as you pause to rest at the site of a station, you can at least in your mind hear echoing along the valley the sound of the whistle from the locomotive of an approaching train.

My thanks to a number of people who read through the text for the book and made suggestions, including Cara Rose, Director of the Pocahontas County Tourism Commission, my wife, Denise, David Caplinger, Superintendent at Seneca State Forest, and Michael Smith, Superintendent at Droop Mountain State Park. However, any mistakes in the book are the responsibility of the author. Suggestions for additional material that should be included and other ways future editions of the book can be made more useful for trail users will be appreciated.

Thanks also go to Roy Shearer, who prepared the list of flowers that can be found along the trail.

For help with the revised edition of this book I want to thank Greenbrier River Trail Superintendent Jody Spencer.

WILLIAM P. MCNEEL
Marlinton, West Virginia

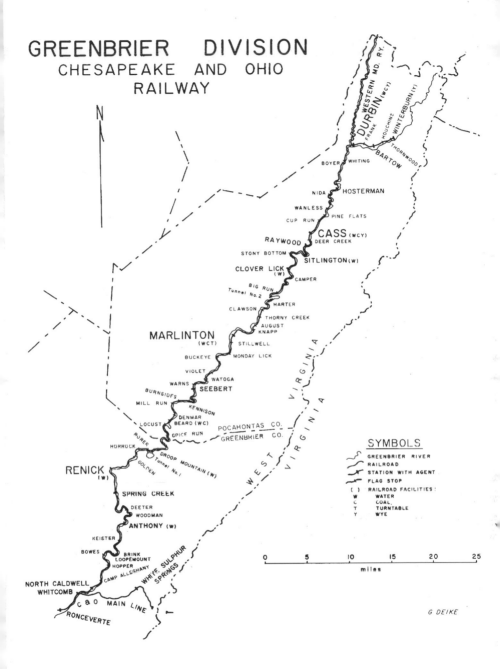

GREENBRIER DIVISION
CHESAPEAKE AND OHIO RAILWAY

N

WESTERN MD. RY.

DURBIN

WINTERBURN (Y)

HOUCHINS

FRANK

WESTERN (WCY)

THORNWOOD

BARTOW

BOYER WHITING

NIDA HOSTERMAN

WANLESS

CUP RUN PINE FLATS

RAYWOOD CASS (WCY)

DEER CREEK

STONY BOTTOM SITLINGTON (W)

CLOVER LICK
(W)

CAMPER

BIG RUN

Tunnel No. 2

CLAWSON HARTER

THORNY CREEK

AUGUST
KNAPP

MARLINTON
(WCT)

STILLWELL

BUCKEYE MONDAY LICK

VIOLET

WARNS WATOGA

BURNSIDES SEEBERT

MILL RUN KENNISON

DENMAR
BEARD (WC)

LOCUST

RORES SPICE RUN

HORROCK

Tunnel No. 1

RENICK GOLDEN DROOP MOUNTAIN (W)
(W)

POCAHONTAS CO.
GREENBRIER CO.

WEST
VIRGINIA

VIRGINIA

SPRING CREEK

DEETER
WOODMAN

ANTHONY (W)

KEISTER

BOWES

BRINK
LOOPEMOUNT
HOPPER

CAMP ALLEGHANY

WHITE SULPHUR
SPRINGS

NORTH CALDWELL
WHITCOMB

C & O MAIN LINE

RONCEVERTE

SYMBOLS

〜 GREENBRIER RIVER

RAILROAD

STATION WITH AGENT

FLAG STOP

( ) RAILROAD FACILITIES:
W WATER
C COAL
T TURNTABLE
Y WYE

0   5   10   15   20   25
miles

G DEIKE

3

The Greenbrier River Trail

*T*he Greenbrier River Trail follows its name-sake river for 77 miles in Greenbrier and Pocahontas counties in eastern West Virginia. Today's trail is located on a portion of the right-of-way of the former Greenbrier Division of the Chesapeake and Ohio Railway. Following the abandonment of the line in 1978, the C&O donated the right-of-way to the West Virginia Railroad Maintenance Authority (now the State Rail Authority) to be kept intact for possible future railroad use. The RMA has leased the property to the state's Division of Parks for development as the Greenbrier River Trail.

Being originally a railroad means that the trail is virtually level and ideal for hikers and cyclists of all ages and abilities, as well as horseback riding. With sufficient snow, the trail is excellent for cross country skiing. Since the trail was established it has suffered some blows from the forces of nature. The massive flooding that hit eastern West Virginia in November 1985 caused serious damage to the trail. The repair work from that flood was not completed until 1994, other projects obviously having a higher priority, only to see the trail again damaged by severe flooding in January and May 1996. The 1996 damage was not as bad as in 1985 and restricted to the northern section of the trail. Repair work following the 1996 floods did not take as long as after 1985 and evidence of the floods is hard to find today. At this writing in the spring of 2004, the trail is in good condition.

The priority of repairing flood damage delayed plans for improvements to the facilities for trail users but a number of projects have been completed. Campsites, safe drinking water, and toilets are now provided at several locations along the trail. A portion of the trail has been paved, beginning south of Marlinton and continuing through town. The depot building at Clover Lick, relocated away from the railroad after the station was closed, has been moved back to a site along the trail and restored. The most recent improvement has been the change of the northern trail head closer to Cass and provision of a proper parking area there. Plans for the future include improved parking at five or six trail access points, and landscaping. A section of the trail through Marlinton is being upgraded with lighting and benches.

In 1999 the Greenbrier River Trail was designated as the Millennium Legacy Trail for West Virginia.

INFORMATION

· Superintendent, Greenbrier River Trail, c/o Watoga State Park, Marlinton, WV 24954, 800 CALL-WVA, local calls 799-4087; wvparks.com/greenbrierrivertrail
· Greenbrier River Trail Association, greenbrierrivertrail.com
· Greenbrier County Convention and Visitors Bureau, 111 N. Jefferson Street, Lewisburg, WV 24901; 800 833-2068, local calls 645-1000; greenbrierwv.com
· Pocahontas County Convention and Visitors Bureau, P. O. Box 275,   Marlinton, WV 24954, 800 336-7009, local calls 799-4636; pocahontascountywv.com

EMERGENCY NUMBERS

Ambulance, Fire, Police:
· Greenbrier County, 911
· Pocahontas County, 911
State Police:
· Lewisburg, 647-7600
· Marlinton, 799-4101

Hospitals:
· Greenbrier Valley Medical Center, Fairlea, 647-4411
· Pocahontas Memorial Hospital, Marlinton, 799-7400

Flowers along the Trail

$\mathcal{P}$eople interested in wild flowers will find the Greenbrier River Trail an excellent location to find flowers of all varieties.

During the spring months the following flowers are among those that can be found:

Trout-lily	Purple Trillium
Large-flowered Trillium	Colt's Foot
Wild Bleeding-heart	Spring Beauty
Dutchman's-breeches	Foamflower
Miterwort	Honeysuckle (pink, orange, etc.)
Yellow Pond Lily	Jack-in-the-pulpit
Alumroot	Bluebeard Lily
Lamb's-quarters	Stinging Nettle (Wood, False, etc.)
Skunk Cabbage	Star Chickweed
Wood Anemone	Spotted Wintergreen
Partridgeberry	May Apple
Daisy Fleabane	Solomon's-seal
False Solomon's-seal	Pokeweed
Early Saxifrage	Ramps
Trailing Arbutus	Bluets
Common Blue Violet	Ground-cherry
Virginia Bluebells	Wild Geranium
Creeping Flax	Cleavers
Dwarf Ginseng	Cut-leaved Toothwort

Early Meadow-rue

Water-hemlock

Teaberry

Dandelion

Violet (many colors)

Golden Ragwort

Wild Ginger

Wild Columbine

Sheep Sorrel

Large-flowered Beardtongue

Gray Beardtongue

Dog Tooth Violet

False

Yellow Lady's-slipper

Bloodroot

Twinleaf

Miami-mist

Catnip

Multiflora Rose

Blueberry

Common Buttercup

Marsh Marigold

Sow Thistle

Dutchman's-pipe

Wood-betony

Round-lobed Hepatica

Cow Vetch

Squawroot

Poison Ivy

Hellebore

Showy Orchis

Corn-salad

Bellwort

and others

As the year moves into summer new flowers appear along the trail:

Wild Sarsaparilla

Ragweed

False Hellebore

Starry Campion

Common Nightshade

Bowman's-root

Common Fleabane

Indian-pipe

White Clover

Black Cohosh

Moth Mullein

Bouncing Bet

White Snakeroot

Yarrow

Black Snakeroot

Pigweed

Strawberries

Bladder Campion

Horse Nettle

Ox-eye Daisy

Aster (many varieties)

Turtlehead

Rattlesnake Plantain

White and Yellow Sweet Clover

Goatsbeard

Peppergrass

Queen Anne's Lace

Cow Parsnip

Boneset	Dodder Vine
Mountain Laurel	Elderberry
Poison Ivy	Buttonbush
Common Milkweed	Rough-fruited Cinquefoil
Black-eyed Susan	Coneflowers
Woodland Sunflower	Bur-marigold
Yellow Hawkweed	Hop Clover
Whorled Loosestrife	Butter-and-eggs
Common Mullein	Goldenrod (several varieties)
Golden Alexanders	Common St. Johnswort
Evening Primrose	Birdfoot Trefoil
Witch Hazel	Turk's-cap Lily
Canada Lily	Spotted Touch-me-not
Yellow Touch-me-not	Butterfly-weed
Cardinal-flower	Bee-balm
Curled Dock	Musk Mallow
Spotted Knapweed	Common Burdock
Teasel	Bull Thistle
Lady's-thumb	Swamp Smartweed
Fireweed	Motherwort
Peppermint	Joe-Pye-weed
Ironweed	Virginia Rose
Chicory	Purple-flowering Raspberry
Monkshood	Tall Beeflower
Blue Vervain	Viper's Bugloss
Heal-all	Closed Gentian
Thimbleweed	Cattail
Dewberry	Deptford Pink
Crown Vetch	Mouse-ear Hawkweed
and others	

Reminders

RESPECT PRIVATE PROPERTY: The trail is in the center of a right-of-way that is generally 100 feet wide. Along most of its length, the property on either side is privately owned. If you go off of the right-of-way make sure you are on other publicly owned land. Do not cross fences. Parking is limited at most trail access points, so be careful to park in a way that will not block local traffic. Do not park on the trail.

DO NOT LITTER: Keep the Greenbrier River Trail clean. If you carried it while full, you can certainly carry it empty. Pick up litter left by inconsiderate trail users.

SHOW COURTESY TO OTHER TRAIL USERS: Bicyclists should slow down when approaching hikers and warn them when coming from behind. Use normal rules when passing other cyclists, hikers, and horse riders. Keep to the right except when passing. Hikers and cyclists should yield to horses.

USE THE TRAIL SAFELY: The two tunnels on the trail are not long enough that they become completely dark as you pass through them. However, the floors become dark as you reach the centers of the tunnels, so be very careful. Also, take care on the bridges.

Trail users need to be aware that hunting is allowed from the trail during the state's hunting seasons, beginning in October. Blaze orange should be worn if on the trail during this period.

REMEMBER, THE TRAIL IS MAINTAINED BY THE DIVISION OF PARKS: Most rules that apply at state parks also apply on the Greenbrier River Trail. The most important regulation forbids any motor driven vehicles on the trail.

*T*he Greenbrier Division was for many years a major branch line of the C&O in West Virginia. It combined the features of both branch and main line railroading including passenger trains with first-class service, timed freight trains from Chicago to the east, motive power of all sizes, up to eleven scheduled trains a day, and the usual assortment of wrecks and other operating problems.

It was constructed between 1899 and 1905 for the purpose of providing the transportation needed to develop the vast timber resources of the upper Greenbrier Valley. The timber resource of the valley was well known to lumbermen in the post Civil War period, but was equally well protected from cutting by the lack of transportation. Beginning in the 1870s the white pine along the river and its major tributaries was taken to mills at Ronceverte by use of the river. Log drives down the Greenbrier River were annual affairs for over 30 years. The cutting took place during the fall and winter months and the logs piled along the streams to wait for the high water in the spring. With luck and skill the logs would be in Ronceverte in a few weeks to provide raw material for the mills. However, only a small percentage of the timber available in the Greenbrier Valley could be transported to the mills by water. Most of the vast amount of timber was too far from a large stream. Also, hardwoods did not float well enough. Mills were not located at the timber because of the same lack of transportation for the lumber. The river was used to move rafts of lumber, but this was possible only a few times a year.

The immediate catalyst for the building of the line

by the C&O, following years of railroad plans for the area but with no results, was the plans of another large company, the West Virginia Pulp and Paper Company (now Westvaco). In the late 1800s WVP&P made plans for a paper mill at Covington, Virginia, and to provide much of the pulp that would be needed for its new mill, the company purchased a large acreage of timberland on Cheat Mountain in Pocahontas County. To get the pulp wood to Covington, a railroad was needed and this guarantee of a large customer provided the C&O with the reason to proceed with the construction of a railroad up the Greenbrier River.

Construction began in July 1899 and Cass, the new town being established by WVP&P, was reached in late 1900. Shipment of pulp began in January 1901. WVP&P also put in a large sawmill at Cass to produce lumber from the timber not suitable for pulp. The mill began operation in January 1902. Cass is the northern point on the Greenbrier River Trail. The Greenbrier Division, however, extended further north. It was completed to Durbin in 1902 and on to Winterburn in 1905. At Durbin a connection was made in 1903 with a branch of the Western Maryland Railway, constructed south from Elkins.

With the completion of the two railroad lines, the cutting of the valley's timber was quickly underway and the resulting lumber filled thousands of railroad cars. Entire new towns were established for the large mill operations and the railroads transported the material needs for the people of both the new and existing communities. Two tanneries were located on the C&O and the valley's existing agricultural industry was quick to turn to the railroads for its transportation needs.

People also needed transportation. For passengers, the C&O provided two trains in each direction, connecting with the same number on the WM. Two of the C&O trains had parlor car service, a rarity on branch line passenger trains.

By the early 1920s the original timber in the valley was almost all cut. The last two major sawmills on the Greenbrier Division started up in 1921, but others had long since sawed their last log. As the mills closed, whole towns virtually disappeared and with them business for the railroad. The automobile, truck, and airplane were also beginning to have an impact on railroads during this time. Regardless of these factors, the 1920s were among the busiest years on the Greenbrier line for as local freight decreased, there was increased use of the line for through traffic. The C&O made the Greenbrier Division part of a new routing of shipments between various western and eastern cities. The C&O promoted two trains handling this traffic as the "Durbin Route." To enable larger engines to be used, the line was upgraded during this period.

The Depression eliminated the separate trains of through traffic on the Greenbrier line and more of the local traffic as most of the sawmills were now long gone. The only major customers were the Cass mill and one tannery. In July 1930 passenger service was reduced to one train in each direction. In 1933 the Bartow to Winterburn section of the line was abandoned.

The World War II period saw the final busy years on the Greenbrier Division. Trains of through freight cars returned and wartime restrictions on the use of automobiles brought people back to the passenger trains. Following the war, however, the slow decline in traffic resumed. Although a few new customers located along the line, it could not survive the loss of important sources of business that came with the closing of the

Cass sawmill in 1960 and the Marlinton tannery in 1970. The passenger train made its last run on January 8, 1958. In 1975 the C&O applied to the Interstate Commerce Commission for permission to abandon its Greenbrier Branch (division status had been gone for many years). Permission was granted in 1978 and the last trains on the line ran to Durbin on December 27 and back on December 28. The WM line into Durbin remained for a little longer but it was abandoned in early 1984. The first three miles of the Greenbrier Branch were retained in service for a few years, but were removed in 1986.

As part of the abandonment proceedings the C&O agreed to donate the right-of-way from milepost 3 to Durbin to the State of West Virginia. The State purchased the track from Cass to Durbin to maintain a rail access for the Cass Scenic Railroad. The rail was removed below Cass and this section became the Greenbrier River Trail. The Cass to Durbin track was used for excursion trains in 1984 and 1985 but this came to an end with the disastrous flood in November 1985 which badly damaged the track.

Although most of the Cass to Durbin track remains in its flood-damaged condition, the five miles south of Durbin have been repaired and put back in use by the Durbin and Greenbrier Valley Railroad for its tourist trains.

For a more detailed history of the Greenbrier Division, the author humbly suggests his book, *The Durbin Route*. It can be ordered from him at 810 Second Avenue, Marlinton, WV 24954. Cost is $12.95 plus $2.00 for shipping. West Virginia residents please add 78¢ tax.

Trail Description

$\mathcal{A}$t the agency stations the mileposts given are for the depots. At flagstops the mileposts are the location of the passenger shelter or, if there was no shelter, the station sign, unless otherwise indicated. Station names not in all capital letters never appeared on Greenbrier Division station lists. At these locations and the unnamed sidings the milepost is the switch, unless otherwise indicated. Bridge mileposts are the middle of the bridge. The mileposts give the distance of the station from the Chesapeake and Ohio Railway mainline at Whitcomb.

Side tracks switched from the main line of track for several purposes. Since the Greenbrier Division was a single track railroad, "passing sidings" were needed to allow trains going in the opposite direction to pass each other or to allow a train with a faster schedule to overtake a slower train. Passing sidings were connected to the main track at both ends and on the east side of the main track unless otherwise indicated. For sidings with only one switch, the expression "stub siding" is used. The term "spur" is used to indicate a siding that left the C&O right-of-way. These sidings were used for the loading and unloading of freight cars. Some sidings served only a single customer while others were provided for the use of anyone wanting rail service. When a removal date is not given for a siding, it was in place until the line was abandoned.

Station lists were issued by the C&O several times a year or annually until 1921. This gives a good idea when stations were established or closed during this period. After 1921 the lists are separated by two or more years. A number of stations were closed between the September 1930 list and the succeeding September 1934 list. The first list with Greenbrier Division stations is dated January 1901.

An "agency" station refers to one where the railroad had a manned depot to provide service to the public and a place where operating instructions could be passed on to train crews. When the Greenbrier Division was constructed, the form of communication between the Division train dispatcher, located at Ronceverte, and the stations was the telegraph. In small communities one person handled all the various duties at a station— agent, telegrapher, ticket seller, clerk, freight and baggage handler, and whatever else had to be done. Stations in larger towns had several employees. The Durbin depot, which handled freight and passenger business of two railroads, had eight employees at one time. At Marlinton a separate freight depot was built and had its own staff. Since traffic on the Greenbrier line was all during the day in the early years, the depots were open only in the daytime. During the peak traffic years of the 1920s and during World War II, a few stations had two or more shifts for train operation purposes.

At "flagstops" the passenger trains stopped for passengers with tickets to these locations and upon signal by a person waiting to board the train. Orders for freight cars at flagstops were handled by the nearest agency station.

The C&O, like most railroads, had standard plans for the structures located along its tracks. The original Greenbrier line depots were all of the same exterior design with identical interior layout—waiting room, office, and freight room—and varied only in length. The office had the traditional bay window to allow a view of the tracks. Most flagstops had one of two types of shelters.

15

One was just a three-sided shelter. The other included a closed room to protect freight.

The section foreman houses were also of the same design. They were L-shaped, and 44–46 feet on the front, 40–42 feet on the side and 16 feet on the ends. (A section foreman was in charge of a crew of men and responsible for track maintenance along a number of miles of track. Greenbrier Division sections were originally ten miles in length.) The bunk houses varied in size but about half were 31.5 by 15.5 feet. Some had additions added. These probably were originally used as quarters for train and track crews, but most became homes rented to railroad employees.

Other structures along the Greenbrier line included one turntable (at Marlinton), several water tanks to provide locomotive water, several facilities to provide coal for locomotives, tool houses for track crews, stock pens for holding animals prior to shipping, and a variety of miscellaneous structures.

Along the trail are concrete markers with the letter "W." These are whistle posts and reminded the engineer to blow the whistle as the train approached either a road crossing or a station. A few speed limit signs also remain. These are circular metal signs, painted yellow with a black number. A sign painted green indicated a train could resume the maximum speeds allowed on the Greenbrier line, which were 25 for freight trains and 35 for passenger trains.

The circular concrete structures at the end of many of the bridges held barrels filled with water to be used if a hot cinder from a passing locomotive caught ties or bridge stringers on fire.

NOTE: *The right-of-way for the first three miles of the former railroad line has been sold to private parties and is not part of the trail.*

WHITCOMB: Milepost 0, elevation 1,701.

Whitcomb was the junction of the Greenbrier Division with the main line of the Chesapeake and Ohio. A depot with a switch tower built on its roof was located at the junction. The name of the junction came from H. D. Whitcomb, a C&O official.

Bridge: Milepost 0.15.

Passing Siding: Milepost 0.33 (south switch).

A passing siding 3,158 feet in length was located a short distance from the junction. It was probably used mainly during the construction period and was removed before 1916.

Bridge: Milepost 0.69.

Little Sulphur Branch bridge: Milepost 1.74.

NORTH CALDWELL (LITTLE SULPHUR, HUNTER): Milepost 1.82, elevation 1,693.

Agency station and telegraph office with call NH. The depot still exists and measures 16.5×61.5 feet. Its

North Caldwell depot. GLEMA AULDRIDGE

17

original position was on the west side of the track just south of the existing road crossing.

The telegraph office was closed in January 1932. After the agency was closed in 1967, the depot building was moved a short distance from the railroad and is now used commercially.

This station appeared on the original Greenbrier station list as Little Sulphur. In September 1901 the depot building was completed and the name of the station was changed to Hunter, for the grantors of the right-of-way in the area. With the station list issued in July 1902, the named was changed again, to North Caldwell, due to confusion with a station called Hunter on the Norfolk and Western Railway.

Other facilities here included a section foreman's house, bunk house, section tool house, and stock pens. For a number of years the railroad operated a farm and nursery at North Caldwell.

A passing siding 3,282 feet in length was located at this station. It was reduced in length on the east end at two different times, leaving a siding of 1,896 feet. The first reduction of 391 feet was done between 1916 and 1926. The second reduction in length was carried out in November 1940. A 1908 track chart and early schedules indicate that there was a stub siding switching from the passing track. Perhaps 190 feet long, it was connected on the south end and gone by 1916; probably removed in early 1910.

North Caldwell was the site briefly considered by the West Virginia Pulp and Paper Company for its new paper mill. A map dated 1899 shows the mill located in the large field upstream of present Rt. 60. To serve the mill a yard complex of five tracks was proposed. One track was to be west of the main track and the others to the east. Several spurs left the easternmost yard track to serve the mill.

HISTORICAL: Existing today are the depot building, relocated as mentioned above, and the section house.

Interstate Amiesite Plant: Milepost 2.82 (south switch).

Two sidings to serve the asphalt plant of the Interstate Amiesite Company (later owned by Anderson Paving, Inc.) were installed in the summer of 1948. Located on the east side of the main track, one was a 957-foot siding connected on both ends. The second was a 340-foot stub siding switching from the first siding and between it and the main track. It was connected on the south end and removed in July 1976.

BRICK YARD (STONE HOUSE): Milepost 2.90 (switch).

A siding about 200 feet long was located here. It was on the east side of the main track and connected on the south end. This station was first on the station list for April 1902 and was not listed in July 1912.

The siding was gone by 1916; probably removed in early 1912.

The original name came from a still-existing home on the hill above the trail. The name change to Brick Yard was made on the April 1906 station list and came from the Greenbrier Brick Company's plant at this location.

Beginning point for 1978 abandonment, End of Track 1978–1986: Milepost 3.06.

Southern Trail Head: Milepost 3.13.

ACCESS: From the east on I-64. Take exit 175, turn left (west) on US Rt. 60, go 2.7 miles to Stone House Road (Co. Rt. 38) at west end of Greenbrier River bridge, 1.3 miles to trail head.

From the west on I-64. Take exit 169, turn left (north) on US Rt. 219, go 0.5 mile to Brush Road (Co. Rt. 30), then 0.5 mile to Stone House Road, and 3 miles to the trail.

From the north on US Rt. 219. Take Brush Road and go as above. From the south on US Rt. 219. Turn right (east) on US Rt. 60 in Lewisburg, then 3 miles to Stone House Road.

FACILITIES: A small parking lot, picnic area, and water are at the trail head. Food, gas, lodging, medical services, and full range of stores available in the Lewisburg area. Camping is available at Greenbrier State Forest (800 CALL-WVA, local calls 536-1944), located off of I-64 at exit 175. Hospital located at Fairlea on US Rt. 219 south of Lewisburg.

AREA ATTRACTIONS: Lewisburg is the oldest established community in the Greenbrier Valley and has many 18th and 19th century buildings. The central part of the town has been designated as a National Historic District. Lewisburg is also the location of the West Virginia School of Osteopathic Medicine. The world famous Greenbrier Resort is located at White Sulphur Springs, east of Lewisburg. Other attractions in the area are a federal fish hatchery at White Sulphur and two commercial caves. In addition to camping, Greenbrier State Forest has hiking trails, a pool, and recreational facilities.

CAMP ALLEGHENY (TOTTENS): Milepost 3.54.

A new station on the station list for December 1923. A shelter shed, 10×10 feet, was built here the previous July. The name was changed to Camp Allegheny in December 1940 for the still operating youth camp of the same name, located across the river from this station. The station was discontinued for freight purposes in November 1956 but remained a passenger flagstop. The first name was from an adjoining landowner, T. K. Totten.

A 642-foot spur was constructed here in 1923 for Cotton and Hanlon. It was east of the main track and connected on the south end. The spur was removed in August 1939.

Intake for Lewisburg water plant: Milepost 3.79.

Campsite: Milepost 4.69, with toilet.

HOPPER: Milepost 5.55.

A 580-foot spur was built here in 1901 for H. W. Hopper. It was east of the main track and connected on the south end. The spur was removed in January 1938 but Hopper was on the freight station list until November 1956. It remained a flagstop for passenger trains until the end of passenger service.

ACCESS: From southern trail head. Take Stone House Road 2 miles to Anderson Road (Co. Rt. 38/2), then 1.1 miles to Harper Road (Co. Rt. 30/3), turn right and go 1.9 miles to the trail. Parking space is limited.

From US Rt. 219. Take Brush Road (Co. Rt. 30) 1.9 miles to Harper Road, then 2.6 miles to the trail.

BOWES: Milepost 7.29.

This station appeared on the station list for October 1903. In 1920 a 391-foot siding was built here for W. O. Slusser. It was on the west side of the main track, connected on the south end, and removed in 1923.

Bowes was on the station list for September 1930 but not on the next list, September 1934. The station name came from a right-of-way grantor, J. H. Bowes.

Bridge: Milepost 7.56.

LOOPEMOUNT: Milepost 8.71.

This station was established in 1925 and 10×9 foot shelter shed erected in the summer of that year. A summer camp was located across the river from this stop. Loopemount was discontinued as a freight station in November 1956 but remained as a passenger flagstop.

There is no evidence that a siding was located at Loopemount.

HISTORICAL: Site of this station is marked by remains of the concrete edge of the station platform.

BRINK: Milepost 9.32.

Station established with the construction of a 549-

foot long spur for the mill of the Clear Creek Lumber Company (c. 1906–c. 1908). It was east of the main track and connected on the south end. The station first appeared on the January 1907 station list.

Sixty feet of the spur were removed in late 1912 or early 1913 and the remainder in April of 1926. Brink was not on the station list issued in January of that year.

KEISTER: Milepost 11.09.

A station building, 10×18.5 feet, was provided at this site, probably of the type with an open passenger shelter and a freight room.

One of the original stations on the line, Keister was discontinued as freight station in November 1956 but remained on the passenger timetable. The station name was from members of the Keister family, right-of-way grantors. Other facilities here included a section foreman's house, bunk house, and section tool house.

A passing siding 2,430 feet in length was located at Keister. In February 1935 the north end of the siding was removed, reducing it to a stub siding 399 feet long. This siding was removed in October 1963.

ACCESS: From US Rt. 219 south of Maxwelton, take Benedict Lane (Co. Rt. 219/19) 2.9 miles to Brush Road (Co. Rt. 30), cross Rt. 30 to Kister Road (Co. Rt. 30/1), then 2 miles to the trail. Limited parking space.

Twelve miles of track were laid by May 1, 1900.

Bridge: Milepost 12.53.

Campsite: Milepost 13.00, with well and toilet.

HISTORICAL: Slides in this area were a constant problem for the railroad. Note the remains of one at the campsite.

Spur: Milepost 13.74.

Location of a spur track of unknown length, leaving the railroad right-of-way after 225 feet. It was on the east side of the main track and connected on the north

Anthony depot, about 1915. COHS

end. The spur was removed by 1916. This is the probable
location of the sawmill operated by Miller-Crozier Lumber
Company (1910–1912). The Miller-Crozier spur was
removed by June 1913.

Dodson Branch bridge: Milepost 13.76.

ANTHONY: Milepost 14.12, elevation 1,796.

Agency station and telegraph office with call HY. The
depot building here was 15.5×58.5 feet and located west
of the track just south of the lower (private) road crossing
in Anthony. The agency/telegraph office was closed in
September 1928 but the building continued in use as the
Anthony post office. The depot was replaced with a
shelter shed in May 1939. Due to increased traffic during
World War II the railroad re-established a telegraph office
at Anthony (call AY) and replaced the shed with a small
building. The telegraph office was closed after the war.

Anthony was one of the original stations established in 1901. S. I. Fleshman moved from the Marlinton station early that year to open the agency here and remained the agent until the Anthony station was closed in 1928. His was the longest tenure of any Greenbrier Division agent.

Other railroad facilities here included a water tank, section foreman's house, bunk house, and section tool house.

A passing siding 2,997 feet long was located at Anthony. It was shortened on the south end to 2,854 feet some time between 1916 and 1926. A 797-foot spur switched off of the passing siding to serve the mill of the Henderson Lumber Company (later Greenwah Lumber Company) (1903–?). The spur was built under a 1904 contract with the lumber company. In 1927 the spur was

On December 28, 1978, the last train ran on the C&O's Greenbrier line. In this photo the train is passing through Anthony, on its way from Durbin to Hinton. PHOTO BY THE AUTHOR

reduced in length to 405 feet and relocated parallel to the main track. It was removed in December 1936.

By early 1943 a 471-foot stub siding was located on the site of the previous siding. It was removed in July 1976. Both sidings were connected on the south end.

Anthony was removed from the list of freight stations in February 1974. Anthony is supposed to have been an Indian who was friendly with the early European settlers in the area.

ACCESS: To reach Anthony from US Rt. 219, take the Anthony Road (Co. Rt. 21) at Frankford. The road to Anthony becomes Co. Rt. 21/2 en route. A parking area for the trail at the river bridge is 4 miles from Rt. 219. Rt. 21/2 continues from Anthony to a connection with WV Rt. 92.

FACILITIES: Gas, groceries, and public phone are available at Frankford. Public access to the river at the Rt. 21/2 bridge. Camping, swimming, and picnicking are available at the USFS Blue Bend Recreation Area 4 miles east of Anthony on Rt. 21/2. Blue Bend is also accessible by Anthony Creek Trail (TR618) and Blue Bend Loop Trail (TR614). The trail begins at the end of the bridge across the river from Anthony and it is 5.3 miles to Blue Bend. There are camp sites along the river at the beginning of the Anthony Creek Trail. The trail crosses Anthony Creek 0.6 mile from the bridge and can be difficult to ford in times of high water.

HISTORICAL: The railroad bunk house has been moved a short distance to a site along the road, west of town. Now a private residence, it had been used as a store. The abutments for the original road bridge across the river are visible north of the present bridge. Most of the Anthony Creek Trail is located on the grade for the Henderson Lumber Company logging railroad.

WOODMAN: Milepost 16.12.

This station was established in 1906 with the building of a sawmill by the Donaldson Lumber Company (1906–1917). A 12.5×28.5 foot freight and passenger structure was located here, replaced by 1938 with a 8×10 foot shelter shed, as well as a bunk house.

A 2,240-foot stub siding, connected on the south end, was built in 1906 to serve the mill. The lumber company railroad was narrow gauge and the siding had a third rail for part of its length to allow equipment of both gauges to operate over it. The siding, located on the east side of the main track, was reduced in length to 760 feet in 1918 and removed in October 1931.

HISTORICAL: Piers for the lumber company bridge can be seen in the river as well as concrete mill foundation in the yards of some of the camps.

Siding: Milepost 16.83.

A stub siding about 350 feet in length was located here, connected on the south end and on the east side of the main track. It was abandoned by 1916.

DEETER: Milepost 17.01 (switch).

This station was established as of the January 1907 station list and was the site of the mill of the Kendall Deeter Lumber Company (1906–c. 1913). The station was not listed on the April 1914 station list.

The mill, located across the river from the railroad, was served by a spur to the east of the main track. The spur had a third rail for most of its length and was connected on the north end. It was gone by 1916; probably removed in 1914 when the station was discontinued.

Eighteen miles of track were in place by the end of May 1900.

Bridge: Milepost 19.11.

Bridge: Milepost 19.22.

GARDNER: Milepost 19.30.

The station appeared on the station list for June 1919 and was no longer listed in 1934. The station lists indicate there was a siding at this point but no details have been found. The name of the station is from Albert Gardner, right-of-way grantor.

Campsite: Milepost 20.52, with toilet.

SPRING CREEK: Milepost 21.53, elevation 1,858.

An agency station and one of the original Greenbrier Division stations. A depot building, 16.5×46 feet, was located about 470 feet south of the bridge over Spring Creek and west of the main track. This building was constructed in 1906. Information on a previous structure has not been found. The agency was closed in 1955. The depot was removed in April 1959 and replaced with a shelter shed. Other facilities here included a section foreman's house, bunk house, and section tool house.

The passing track here was 3,211 feet long in 1901. By 1916 it had been shortened on the south end and was 2,941 feet long. A further reduction in length to 2,715 feet was made in late 1921 when the mill of the Spring Creek Lumber Company (1921–1934) was under construction. This reduction was on the north end and was to allow the lumber company's logging railroad from Spring Creek to cross the Chesapeake and Ohio line to reach the mill. In the spring of 1937 the passing track was replaced with a 652-foot stub siding, connected on the south end.

Two spurs were built from the passing track to serve the mill, both connected on the north end. However, one was not used and soon removed. The other was taken out in the spring of 1937.

After the closing of the Spring Creek mill, the mill site was occupied by the mill of the S. J. Neathawk Lumber Company (later Greenbrier Lumber Company).

View of Spring Creek soon after the track was completed to this point. A construction train is on the bridge and a train of camp cars, which provided housing for construction crews, is on a temporary siding. The bridge in the photo was temporary and replaced by a steel structure. PAULINE WOLFENBARGER

Photo showing the mill of the Spring Creek Lumber Company. PCHS

Under its contract with the railroad on the crossing, the lumber company was required to install and maintain safety signals to protect the traffic on the main track. Four were installed, two near the crossing and two about a half-mile away, on each side.

ACCESS: The Spring Creek Station Road (Co. Rt. 13) connects with US Rt. 219 at Renick (for those coming south) and 1 mile north of Frankford (for northbound travellers). Spring Creek is 3 miles from Renick and 2 miles from the other Rt. 219 intersection. Parking space for trail users is limited at Spring Creek.

HISTORICAL: The grade for the Spring Creek Lumber Company railroad leaves the trail a short distance south of the bridge. The two small concrete foundation blocks in this area do not exactly fit track map notations, but are probably bases for signals.

Spring Creek bridge: Milepost 21.65.

Present bridge installed in 1929.

HISTORICAL: The concrete structure at MP 22.75 is a base for a well house used by track workers.

One of the most difficult areas of construction on the railroad was the cliff north and south of MP 24. The cliff consists of limestone from the Greenbrier Series, one of the more important geological formations in the Greenbrier Valley. The fine grazing lands known as the "Big Levels" of Greenbrier County and the "Little Levels" of Pocahontas County were both developed in this rock formation by a geologically earlier version of the Greenbrier River. Some of the largest cave systems in West Virginia exist in this limestone and the formation has been an important source of limestone rock. The Greenbrier Series is exposed along the trail from this cliff to the old quarry north of Renick. The two small openings at the base of the cliff along the trail do not open into caves.

Construction work on the new railroad near Renick. PAULINE WOLFENBARGER

RENICK: Milepost 24.77, elevation 1,873.

One of the original stations and an agency station and telegraph office with call RN, later RW. A station building, 16.5×71 feet, was located south of the road crossing and west of the track. It was completed in September 1900. Freight service was available to Renick by the middle of July 1900. The Renick agency was closed in 1966 and the building removed the same year.

Other railroad facilities here included a section foreman's house, bunk house, section tool house, water tank, and stock pens.

A passing siding of 3,510 feet, east of the main track, and a loading siding of 2,188 feet, west of the main track, were located at Renick. The loading track was originally a stub siding about 1,300 feet long, connected on the south end. It was lengthened and a second switch added by 1908. Both of these tracks were reduced in length on the north end in November 1940 to 2,507 and 1,284 feet respectively. The passing track was removed in July 1976.

In 1925 a 354-foot spur was built to serve a Standard Oil Company bulk plant. The siding switched from the passing track and was connected on the north end. It was removed by early 1933.

The Horrocks Desk Company (1904–c. 1925) had a factory in Renick, located along the loading siding just north of Milepost 25.

The incorporated name of the community is Falling Springs but the railroad chose the name of a pioneer family in the area for the name of its station.

ACCESS: The trail is a short distance from US Rt. 219 by way of the Auto Road (Co. Rt. 11).

FACILITIES: Boat launching ramp near the trail; gas, groceries, and public phone on Rt. 219.

HISTORICAL: Railroad remains are the foundation

Waiting for the passenger train at Renick. Judging by the good clothes being worn by most of the people on the platform, they are going on some type of special excursion. Date unknown. PCHS

Tipple at the Renick Stone Company quarry, 1928. WENDELL A. SCOTT

for the water tank and the concrete pump house, located at the north end of Renick.

Renick Stone Company: Milepost 25.82 (tipple).

The tipple of the Renick Stone Company (1907–1940s) was served by three tracks. Two were stub sidings connected to the main track at their north ends. One was 361 feet long. The other was originally 1,257 feet long, then 1,131 feet, and finally 1,331 feet in length. The third siding, 343 feet long, switched off of the longer of the other two tracks and was connected at both ends. A short stub siding, about 125 feet long was connected to the longer siding but removed by 1916. The sidings were laid in 1907 and removed in February 1955.

HISTORICAL: Foundations for the quarry tipple as well as the large quarry can be seen.

DeHART: Milepost 26.27 (switch).

A 263-foot stub siding was built at this location in 1920 for S. D. DeHart on the east side of the main track. It was connected on the south end. The siding was removed in 1925 and the name no longer on the January 1926 issue of the station list. DeHart was first listed in July 1921.

Bridge: Milepost 27.66.

GOLDEN: Milepost 28.19.

Site of a small sawmill operated by Paul Golden (1917–?). A station with his name first appeared in the January 1918 station list

A spur, 828 feet in length, was built in 1917 to serve the mill. It was east of the main track and connected on the south end. The spur was removed in 1925 but Golden was a freight station until November 1956 and remained passenger flagstop until the end of that service.

Campsites: Mileposts 28.46 and 28.52, with well, toilet, and horse rail.

Twenty-nine miles of track were laid by July 1, 1900.

Bridge: Milepost 29.42.

Bens Run bridge: Milepost 29.61.

HORROCK: Milepost 29.64.

This station appeared on the station list in July 1903 and a 10.5×16.5 station building was provided here. It was removed in early 1937.

A stub siding of 435 feet was built here in 1904 for the Horrocks Desk Company. It was west of the main track and connected on the south end. It was not used by the company after 1909 but remained in place until November 1935.

The station was removed from the freight station list in November 1956 but remained as a passenger flagstop.

ACCESS: To reach Horrock from US Rt. 219 take Brownstown Road (Co. Rt. 7) in Renick (for those coming north) or 2.6 miles from the Greenbrier/Pocahontas County line (for those traveling south). Horrock/Rorer Road (Co. Rt. 7/2) is 5.2 miles from Renick, then 0.4 mile to the trail. By the other route, go 1.3 miles, turn left at the intersection, and then 1.2 miles to Rt. 7/2. The road into Horrock is not paved and parking is limited.

Rt. 7/2 continues on to Rorer, but there is no parking available beyond Horrock.

HISTORICAL: At milepost 30.14 there was a grist mill when the railroad was constructed. The remains of the mill dam can be seen in the river and along the edge of the road below the trail there is a stone foundation for the mill.

Bridge: Milepost 30.57.

RORER: Milepost 30.62 (originally 30.83).

A 32-foot boxcar body was provided here to shelter freight and passengers. It was removed in October 1957.

The station appeared on the station list for October 1901 with the building of a 279-foot stub siding under a contract with P. H. Rorer. It was east of the main track and connected on the north end. Rorer was removed from the freight station list in November 1956 but the siding was not removed until the late summer of 1976. It was a flagstop until the end of passenger service.

Spur: Milepost 30.88.

Switch for a spur track to the east to serve the sawmill of the Grove City Lumber Company (1904–1915). The spur was completed by April 1905 and removed by 1916.

The mill town was called Greenbrier but this name never appeared on a station list or timetable.

On February 8, 1905, snow got too deep for a freight train and a passenger train near Droop Mountain and their trip south ended until the next day. RUTH SHARP BEEBE

Droop Mountain Tunnel: Milepost 30.91 (south portal). This tunnel is 402 feet long.

The tunnel was completed by May 1900.

HISTORICAL: At each end of the tunnel there is a pole with an arm that has rope hanging from the arm. These are "tell tales" to warn a brakeman riding the top of a car that the tunnel is near.

DROOP MOUNTAIN: Milepost 32.10.

This station appeared on the original station list for the Greenbrier line. Railroad facilities here included a water tank, section foreman's house, and section tool house. The station was removed in November 1956 from the list of freight stations but remained a passenger flagstop.

A 3,240-foot passing siding was located here. It was removed in January 1937. The Hogg Lumber Company (1905–?) had a sawmill at or near this station.

HISTORICAL: The only evidence for the Droop Mountain station is foundation remains for the section foreman's house in the woods above the trail.

Campsite: Milepost 32.12. The weathering of sandstone has provided a sandy "beach" for this campsite.

Bridge: Milepost 32.22.

Campsite: Milepost 33.67, with toilet.

HISTORICAL: The grade for the Spice Run Lumber Company railroad to Davy Run can be seen across the river from the campsite.

Siding: Milepost 35.13.

A 328-foot stub siding was located here, west of the main track, connected on the north end. It was probably used by the Spice Run Lumber Company and was abandoned before 1916.

Greenbrier/Pocahontas county line: Milepost 35.45.

Siding: Milepost 35.87.

Location of a stub siding 280 feet in length on the west side of the main track and connected on the south end. It was installed for the Little Creek Lumber Company and removed in late 1912 or early 1913.

Bridge: Milepost 36.02.

SPICE RUN: Milepost 36.02 (1913 and after).

The Spice Run station appeared on the station list in April 1902. Exact location of the original station is not known; probably the name for the siding at MP 35.87.

In 1913 the Spice Run Lumber Company (1913–c. 1926) located a sawmill at this site. While the mill was in operation the railroad ticket office was in the lumber company store which was located along the track.

Although not an agency station, there was a ticket agent here from 1914 to 1928. A shelter shed was provided in later years.

To serve the mill a 1,651-foot passing siding was installed with two spurs into the mill complex. Coming from the south the first spur, 594 feet long, was connected on the north end and provided access to the mill

Spice Run Lumber Company sawmill at Spice Run. This view of the mill is from the north. PCHS

yard and the lumber company bridge across the river. The other, connected on the south end and 922 feet long, went to the mill and log pond. The first siding was removed in 1925 and the second in 1928. The passing track was removed in February 1935.

The Vulcan Last Company (?–c. 1927) had a plant across the river from Spice Run and was served by the lumber company railroad. (Lasts were forms shaped like a foot used in shoemaking.)

Spice Run was removed from the freight station list in November 1956 but continued as a passenger flagstop.

HISTORICAL: The piers for the lumber company bridge and the site of the sawmill can be seen on the east side of the trail.

Siding: Milepost 36.66.

Stub siding of about 190 feet in length on the west side of the main track, connected on the south end. It was removed by 1916. This siding may have been installed in late 1913 for the Lilly Lumber Company.

LOCUST (BREAKNECK): Milepost 37.40 (originally 37.36).

A 12×12 foot building described as a freight house was located at this station.

Breakneck appeared on the station list for July 1904 with the construction of a 400-foot siding for T. F. Callison, R. Callison and H. A. Slear. It was west of the main track and connected on the south end. The contract for the siding was acquired by the Kidd, Kirby and Lilly Lumber Company (1907–c. 1912) for their mill on Trump Run and lengthened to 900 or more feet. It was shortened to 315 feet by the mid 1920s and removed in April 1935.

The name Breakneck was given this area in the river during the log drive days. Trains were operating to this point by the middle of September 1900. The name was changed from Breakneck to Locust with the station list dated July 1912. Locust came off of the freight station list in November 1956, but remained as a passenger flagstop.

Locust Creek bridge: Milepost 37.57.

Present bridge installed in 1929.

LOCUST: Milepost 37.72 (switch).

Site of a stub siding about 300 feet in length, west of the main track and connected on the south end. It was built in late 1910 for the J. E. Moore Lumber Company (1911–c. 1913). The company's sawmill was on Locust Creek, not at the railroad.

The siding was removed in 1912 or 1915. The name first appeared in the January 1911 list of stations and was no longer at this location on the July 1912 list.

BEARD (BEARDS): Milepost 38.48, elevation 2,010.

An agency station and telegraph office with call BA. The depot building here was two stories high and 16.5×53.5 feet in size. It was on the west side of the track and just south of the present road crossing. The second

View at Beard, looking to the north, showing the unusual two-story depot, water tank, and coaling platform. PCHS

story served as a residence for the agent and his family. The agency/telegraph office was closed in September 1928 and the building removed in April 1937.

Other facilities at Beard included a water tank, coaling platform, stock pens, section foreman's house, section tool house, and, for some reason, four bunk houses.

A passing siding and a 520-foot stub siding were located here.

The passing track was 3,200 feet long in 1901 but shortened on the south end to 2,997 feet by 1916. The stub siding was on the east side of the passing track and connected on the south end. It was laid about 1927 with rail taken from Denmar and removed in December 1936. The passing track was removed in the late summer of 1976.

One of the original stations on the Greenbrier Division, Beard was removed from the list of freight stations in February 1974. The station name came from right-of-way grantors, members of the Beard Family, a pioneer family in the area.

ACCESS: The trail at Beard is on Beard Road (Co. Rt. 31/8), 0.5 mile from the Denmar Road (Co. Rt. 31) Coming northbound on US Rt. 219, take the Locust Creek Road (Co. Rt. 20) 3.1 miles to Rt. 31, then left 1.4 miles to Beard Road. Southbound on US Rt. 219, take Rt. 31 in Hillsboro and then 4.9 miles to Beard Road.

FACILITIES: A bed and breakfast is located at Beard. Gas, restaurant, groceries, public phone and medical clinic are available in Hillsboro.

HISTORICAL: North of the road crossing the foundation for the water tank is on the west side of the trail. On the other side are foundation remains for the pump house and coaling platform as well as a concrete water intake house.

The only remaining covered bridge in Pocahontas County is located at the intersection of Rts. 20 and 31. It was constructed in 1888.

AREA ATTRACTIONS: The birthplace of the author Pearl S. Buck is located in Hillsboro and open to the public. South of Hillsboro on US Rt. 219 are Droop Mountain Battlefield State Park (653-4254), which is the site of the largest Civil War battle in West Virginia, and Beartown State Park. Facilities at Droop include picnic areas, trails, and a small museum. Beartown is a natural area with interesting rock formations.

WV Rt. 39 West, two miles north of Hillsboro, provides access to the Cranberry Wilderness Area, Cranberry Back Country, the Cranberry Glades Botanical Area, Falls of Hills Creek, and the southern end of the Highland Scenic Highway (WV Rt. 150). Information on this section of the Monongahela National Forest is available at the U. S. Forest Service Cranberry Mountain Visitor Center (653-4826), 7 miles east of Rt. 219.

DENMAR (DEN MAR): Milepost 39.33.

Station established in 1910 with the building of a

View of Denmar showing the town, lumber yard, and mill of the
Maryland Lumber Company. Located on the site of the town today
is the former hospital building now used for a minimum security
prison. PCHS

sawmill by the Maryland Lumber Company (1910–
1918). The company's store building was located at the
railroad with a platform in front and it served as a passenger depot, freight depot, and express office. Denmar
first appeared on the January 1911 station list.

To serve the mill, a 1,246-foot siding was installed,
connected on both ends and east of the main track. A
spur switched from this to connect with the mill yard
tracks. The siding was changed to a stub siding with the
removal of the north switch and 520 feet of track by
early 1928. In early 1933 the siding was again shortened.
The remaining track, either 309 feet or 431 feet, was
removed in September 1968.

Following the closing of the mill, Denmar was acquired by the State of West Virginia and became the site
of the state hospital for Black people with tuberculosis. It
was later a hospital for the chronically ill before being

closed in 1990. In 1994 the property was re-opened by the state for use as a medium security prison.

Both spellings of the name of this station were used simultaneously. Station lists consistently used Den Mar while schedules usually had Denmar. Den is from lumber company president J. A. Denison and Mar from Maryland.

HISTORICAL: The piers for the lumber company bridge can be seen in the river.

MILL RUN: Milepost 40.89.

A 16×24 foot building described as a freight house was located here.

Mill Run was the junction with the logging railroad of the Spice Run Lumber Company that ran to Hills Creek. It appeared on the station list for August 1915, the year the logging road was built. The switch to the logging line was removed in 1925.

Mill Run was on the September 1930 station list but was closed before the next edition, September 1934. In 1946 the passenger trains were again authorized to use Mill Run as a flagstop.

Campsite: Milepost 40.89, with horse rail. The campsite is located on the logging railroad grade.

Mill Run bridge: Milepost 40.91.

BURNSIDES: Milepost 41.70.

A 8.5×10.5 foot shelter shed was provided here for passengers.

A 342-foot spur was installed here in 1901 under a contract with T. A. Sydenstricker, C. L. Clarke, and F. W. Harper. It was on the west side of the main track and connected on the south end. In July 1923, 99 feet were removed and the balance taken out in April 1935.

Burnsides was removed from the freight station list in November 1956 but remained a passenger flagstop. The name is from right-of-way grantors, members of the Burnside Family, descendants of one of the early settlers in the region.

ACCESS: From US Rt. 219 at Hillsboro take the Denmar Road 1.2 mile to the Workman Road (Co. Rt. 31/1), then 1.1 miles to the trail. The pavement ends at 0.6 mile; stay straight at this point. Limited parking space.

Harper Run bridge: Milepost 41.71.

KENNISON: Milepost 42.42 (switch).

Location of a siding built in 1917 under contract with the Maryland Lumber Company. It was 430 feet long, connected on the south end, and east of the main track. F. P. Kidd acquired timber across the river from the Maryland Lumber Company and installed a sawmill at this site (1918–c. 1923). The siding was removed in 1925.

Kennison appeared in the station list for January 1918. After the mill ceased operation, the flagstop was moved to milepost 42.95

The station was eliminated from the railroad's list of freight stations in November 1956 but was retained as a passenger flagstop. Name from a right-of-way grantor, A. R. Kennison. Charles and Jacob Kennison were among the pre-Revolutionary War settlers of the Hillsboro area.

REXROAD: Milepost 42.47 (switch).

Location of a stub siding about 275 feet in length that served a small sawmill operated by Wilson and Rexroad. The siding was installed in late 1912 or early 1913 and removed by 1916; probably removed in 1914 as Rexroad was not listed on the April 1914 station list. The siding was located west of the main track and connected on the south end.

Rexroad was first listed as a station with the September 1913 list.

ANDREW

A new station on the station list for January 1903 with station number 44, which indicates it was located

Seebert depot after the structure had been increased in length in 1907. PCHS

near MP 44. A stub siding at Milepost 44.57 may have been the location of Andrew.

The siding was 300+ feet long, connected on the east end, and north of the main track. It was gone by 1916 but probably removed in 1906 as Andrew no longer appeared on the July 1906 station list.

SEEBERT: Milepost 45.77, elevation 2,059.

Agency station and telegraph office with call SB. Seebert was one of the original stations on the line and the community's name comes from an early settler, Jacob Seybert. The depot building here was originally 16.5×55 feet. In 1907 the freight room was lengthened by 25 feet. The building was located about 1,000 feet north of the present road crossing, west of the track. The Seebert agency was closed in July 1963 and the depot was sold and removed.

Other railroad facilities at Seebert included stock pens, section foreman's house, bunk house, and section tool house.

The passing siding at Seebert was originally 3,000 feet in length (1901 and 1916). In June 1938 it was reduced in length on the north end to slightly over 1,700 feet. It was extended northward 250 feet in the spring of 1946, making its final length 1,974 feet.

Two stub sidings were located south of the depot on the west side of the main track. One switched from the main track and ran to the depot, 1,419 feet in length. The second siding switched from the first and was built in 1901 under a contract with the Farmers Implement and Supply Company and the Seebert Milling Company. Over the years various lengths are given for this siding, from 581 feet to 611 feet. After World War II, coal mined in the Briery Knob area was loaded into cars on this siding.

To the north of the depot a 553 foot (later 600) stub siding switched from the main track and ran to the depot. It was built in 1901 under a contract with S. J. Payne and was removed in June 1938.

ACCESS: The intersection of US Rt. 219 and the Seebert Road (Co. Rt. 27) is between Hillsboro and Mill Point. The trail is 1.9 miles from Rt. 219.

Seebert can also be reached from WV Rt. 39 by taking the Beaver Creek Road (Co. Rt. 21) at Huntersville, then 7.3 miles to the northern entrance to Watoga State Park, (Co. Rt. 21/4) and 6.6 miles through the park to the trail.

FACILITIES: A convenience store, with bike and canoe rentals, and lodging are available at Seebert. Camping, cabins, trails, pool, lake, recreation areas, and restaurant are available in Watoga State Park, across the river from Seebert. The park's river campground is 1.5 miles from the trail and the restaurant and park headquarters are 4.3 miles. Gas, restaurant, groceries, public phone, and medical clinic are available in Hillsboro.

HISTORICAL: The site of the Seebert depot is marked

by a concrete foundation for a signal. Watoga State Park is one of the facilities in West Virginia that was developed by the Civilian Conservation Corps. Two CCC camps were in the park and most of the park buildings are CCC constructed. A small CCC museum is located in the park.

Bridge: Milepost 45.84.

Bridge: Milepost 46.14.

WARNS: Milepost 46.32.

Junction with the Cranberry Railroad, the logging railroad for the Warn Lumber Company (1905–1913). The sawmill was located on Stamping Creek about a half mile from the C&O. The logging line had a 1,380-foot siding for interchange of cars, connected on both ends, a short distance from the junction. The junction was installed in 1905 and removed in 1917.

The Warn railroad also served the mill of John Raine and Company (1907–1914), located farther up Stamping Creek, about five miles from the junction.

Warns did not appear on station lists until the January 1913 edition and was no longer on the June 1919 list.

Stamping Creek bridge: Milepost 46.42.

The track was in place to this point by the middle of October 1900. Present bridge installed in 1929. The name is supposed to be from the stamping of buffalo that once lived in the area.

Stephen Hole Run bridge: Milepost 46.98.

Present bridge installed in 1929. The name comes from a small cave at the head of the stream that is believed to have been lived in by Stephen Sewell for a winter (about 1750). Limited parking at road crossing.

Greenbrier River bridge: Milepost 47.90.

One span of the present bridge dates to 1925 and the other to 1929.

WATOGA: Milepost 48.10.

Aftermath of a wreck at the bridge across the river at Watoga on May 4, 1925. A derailed box car in a northbound freight train hit the end of the bridge and caused one span to fall into the river. PCHS

A passenger station, 16.5×30.5 feet, was located in the "S" curve on the east side of the main track and a lumber company siding. Built in 1907, it was similar in appearance to a standard depot building but had no bay window. The building was probably constructed by the lumber company and not the railroad. It was gone by the late 1930s and replaced with a shelter shed.

Watoga was the location of a sawmill owned in succession by the J. R. Droney, Tomb, and Watoga Lumber Companies (1906–c. 1916). The Empire Kindling Wood Company also had a plant here (1908–?). The siding connecting the railroad to the tracks serving the mill and kindling plant left the main line north of the depot. It was installed in 1906 and removed by 1930.

A logging railroad switched from the siding at the depot, ran parallel to the main track to Violet, and then went up Beaver Creek.

View of the town of Watoga showing the sawmill in the right of the photo and the kindling wood plant in the center of the photograph. PCHS

Watoga first appeared on the station list for July 1906. The station was briefly referred to as ISLAND LICK. The name Watoga may have been an Indian word but it also may have been a created word with no meaning.

HISTORICAL: The foundation for the lumber company's store building is visible along the trail. Remains of the company safe are part of the foundation.

VIOLET (DAN): Milepost 49.24.

Two sidings were located here. One was on the west side of the main track, connected on the south end, and 564 feet long. It was removed in February 1938. This siding was built in 1901 for the West Virginia Pulp and Paper Company.

The other siding was on the east side of the main track, connected on the south end, and 225 or more feet in length. It was removed before 1916.

A telegraph office may have been located here for a brief period of time immediately following the construction of the railroad.

This station was on the first Greenbrier line schedule as BEAVER CREEK, but changed to Dan on the second schedule. The name was changed to Violet on the June 1906 station list. Dan is from Dan O'Connell, a logging contractor. The origin of the name Violet is not known; perhaps for the flower.

Violet was discontinued for freight purposes in November 1956 but remained a passenger flagstop.

Beaver Creek bridge: Milepost 49.31.

Present bridge installed in 1929.

Campsite: Milepost 49.36, with toilet and horse rail.

Siding: Milepost 50.23.

This 579-foot stub siding was built for the Marlin Lumber Company in December 1928–January 1929. It was east of the main track and connected on the north end. The lumber company railroad on Improvement Lick connected with this siding. Removal date is not known.

Improvement Lick Run bridge: Milepost 50.23.

IMPROVEMENT LICK: Milepost 50.32 (switch).

Location of a siding about 400 feet long, east of the main track and connected on the north end. It was installed in 1902, probably for the Greenbrier River Lumber Company and later served a small sawmill operated by Judson Howard. The siding was removed before 1916, perhaps in 1910 as the station no longer appeared with the September 1910 edition of the station list. It was first listed in October 1902.

Campsite: Milepost 51.41.

Sugar Camp Run bridge: Milepost 51.43.

PETERS: Milepost 51.48 (switch).

Location of a stub siding about 300 feet long on the

east side of the main track and connected on the north end. It was installed in 1902 and removed by 1916, perhaps in 1905 as the name no longer appeared on the station list for April 1905. It was first on the October 1902 list.

In July 1928 a 281-foot stub siding was built on almost the same location for the Marlin Lumber Company, also connected on the north end. The removal date is not known.

BUCKEYE: Milepost 52.18.

One of the original stations on the Greenbrier line, named for the existing community on the other side of the river. A 10.5×19.5 foot passenger shelter/freight room building was provided here, located south of the road crossing. It was reduced to just a passenger shelter by 1943. Although never a full agency station, Buckeye did have a ticket agent for a number of years beginning in 1912.

Other facilities at Buckeye included a section foreman's house and section tool house.

Buckeye was the location of a 2,528-foot passing siding, built on the west side of the main track instead of the more usual east side.

Small station building at Buckeye. PCHS

The passing siding was removed in late 1936. A 929-foot spur switched from the passing track to serve the mill of the American Column and Lumber Company (1914–1917). The spur was removed in 1920.

ACCESS: From US Rt. 219 in Buckeye take the Old Buckeye Road (Co. Rt. 219/5) for a short distance, then right on Buckeye Station Road (Co. Rt. 219/15) 0.5 mile across the river to the trail.

FACILITIES: Groceries, gas, public phone, motel, and medical clinic are available in Buckeye.

HISTORICAL: The Buckeye section house remains in place (with school building adjacent), about 1,200 feet north of the bridge.

Siding: Milepost 52.39.

From the switch a siding extended south 350 feet to the Buckeye passing track. Whether this was a separate side track or indicates the passing track was longer at one time is not known. This track was gone by 1916.

AUMILLER: Milepost 52.65 (switch).

A stub siding about 200 feet long was located at this site in 1904 to serve a sawmill operated by Aaron and Wesley Aumiller (1904–1906). It was east of the main track and connected on the south end. The siding was gone by 1916; probably removed in 1906 as the name was no longer on the April 1906 station list. It was first listed in July 1904.

Milepost 53.06: From here through Marlinton the trail is paved.

Monday Lick Run bridge: Milepost 53.86.

MUNDAY LICK: Milepost 53.92 (switch).

Location of a 450-foot stub siding on the east side of the main track and connected on the north end. The siding crossed Monday Lick on its own bridge. The siding was probably installed for the Greenbrier River Lumber Company which had a camp at this site.

Munday Lick appeared on the October 1902 station list and was gone from the November 1908 list. The siding was gone by 1916 but was probably removed at the time the station was discontinued. The spelling for the stream was probably once the same as the station and is believed to have come from the name of an individual.

HISTORICAL: The grade for the Marlin Lumber Company logging railroad up Monday Lick is visible on the east side of the trail. It ran parallel to the C&O from Stillwell, but much of it was taken out by the existing Forest Service road.

Milepost 54: Entrance to the Wyatt Interpretive Trail, named in honor of Tom Wyatt, a long-time employee of the U. S. Forest Service. The area consists of a short nature trail aimed toward elementary age children. Picnic tables are provided. The Marlin Lumber Company railroad grade continues on up Sunday Lick but is not developed as a trail.

Sunday Lick Run bridge: Milepost 54.07.

Siding: Milepost 54.20.

Stub siding on the west side of the main track. It was about 225 feet long, connected on the north end, and possibly installed for the Greenbrier River Lumber Company. It was removed by 1916.

Siding: Milepost 54.79.

Stub siding of 501 feet to serve the mill of the R. S. Burrus Lumber Company (now Cramer Lumber Company) (1963 to date). Built in April 1964, the siding was connected on the north end and on the west side of the main track.

Stillhouse Run bridge: Milepost 55.03.

STILLWELL: Milepost 55.06.

Site of the mill of the Marlin Lumber Company (1921–1932). The mill was located a short distance up Stillhouse Run from the railroad and a spur, connected on the north end, was built in 1920 to serve the mill yard. The spur was removed by early 1940.

Stillwell was first listed in the July 1921 edition of the station list. It was taken off of the list of freight stations in November 1956 but remained as a flag stop for the passenger train.

Construction work on the grade for the railroad was underway in this area in late August 1899.

ACCESS: The trail is accessible at Stillwell at the Marlinton Municipal Park. The road to the park starts as Fifth Avenue in Marlinton and becomes Co. Rt. 39/2.

FACILITIES: Water, toilets, picnic areas, and recreation facilities are available at the Park. Camping is allowed at the park.

SIDE TRIP: A ten-mile loop can be made by taking Stillhouse Run Road (FR304), across from the park, up to the Allegheny Trail on the top of Buckley Mountain, then Monday Lick Road (FR1002) back to Stillwell.

FR304 is open to vehicles all year and FR1002 in the fall. Cyclists should be experienced before taking this route.

Knapps Creek bridge: Milepost 55.74.

Construction work on the original bridge began in early September 1899. The present bridge was installed

Work was underway on the bridge over Knapps Creek in the fall of 1899. PCHS

53

On October 26, 1900, the people of Marlinton held a grand rally to celebrate the "first train" in their town. The day included a barbecue, tournament, football (soccer), coronation of a queen, ball, and appropriate speakers. The photo was taken near the present Main Street crossing. PCHS

in 1929. The name is said to come from Napthalen Gregory, who is believed to have been one of the first Europeans to come to the Greenbrier Valley.

MARLINTON: Milepost 56.13, elevation 2,128.

Agency station and telegraph office with call MO. The still existing depot building here measures 16.5×76 feet and is located just north of the Eighth Street crossing. As originally constructed, it had three rooms— waiting room, 15.5 feet, agent's office, 12 feet, and freight room, 48.5 feet. The freight room had two doors on each side. A loading platform was built across the back side of the depot and was connected with the trackside platform on the south end of the building.

In late 1905 a separate freight station, 20.5×80.5 feet,

was built north of the depot. After the freight station was built, the passenger depot was altered by shortening the freight room by 22 feet to provide a second waiting room, 19 feet, and to enlarge the office by 3 feet.

The Marlinton depot was completed in February 1901 and in use until the Greenbrier line closed at the end of 1978. The building was donated to a local preservation group and has been restored to its original exterior look on the front side. The building is presently serving as the office and visitor center of the Pocahontas County Convention and Visitors Bureau. The freight station was closed about 1955 and the building removed in late 1976.

Sharing the depot platform is an 18.5×30.5 foot building that was originally a warehouse located across the tracks from the depot. It was moved to its present location in 1913 and converted to an office building. It housed the office of the Greenbrier Division dispatcher

This Greenbrier Division train crew posed its train for a photo at Marlinton, just below the Ninth Street crossing. The date is not known, but it must not be too many years after the line was built judging by the lack of vegetation along the track. COHS

Passenger train arriving at the Marlinton depot, en route to Ronceverte. Photo taken between 1905 and 1913. PCHS

for a few years. It was also used as the office for the Greenbrier track maintenance supervisor as well as a Western Union telegraph office.

Other railroad facilities at Marlinton over the years included a turntable, water tank, coaling trestle, section foreman's house, three bunk houses, section tool houses, motor car house, stock pens, blacksmith shop, supply house, garage, and ashpit.

As might be expected there were a number of tracks in the Marlinton yard and variations in their arrangement over the years. The two major sidings were a loading track west of the main track and a passing track on the east side of the main line. The loading siding's length was 2,820 feet in 1916 and later extended to 3,020 feet. The length of the passing track was 2,010 feet in 1916 and it was later increased in length to 2,700 feet. Other sidings were for the tannery, turntable, and coaling dock.

The track was completed to Marlinton in October 1900 and the town had a "first train" celebration on October 26. Passenger service on the Greenbrier line began on December 17, 1900, with Marlinton as the initial end of the line. Marlinton's name comes from Jacob

As the number of passengers declined in the 1920s and 1930s due to the increasing use of automobiles, the C&O and other railroads began using gas/electric motor cars on many branch-line passenger runs to reduce costs. The motor cars began operating on the Greenbrier line in 1929. This photo was taken in Marlinton on June 26, 1945. CHARLES A. BROWN

Construction work on the grade above Marlinton, 1900. PCHS

Marlin, who settled, with Stephen Sewell, at the site of the town in 1749. Although they were at Marlinton for only a year or two, some sources credit them with being the first European settlers west of the Allegheny Mountain.

ACCESS: The trail passes through Marlinton, crossing WV Rt. 39 (Main Street) at Fourth Avenue.

FACILITIES: Food, gas, lodging, bike and canoe rentals, river access, stores, public phone, banks, ATMs, medical offices, and a hospital (on US 219, 1½ miles south of town) are available in Marlinton. Information is available at the Pocahontas County Convention and Visitors Bureau office at the depot. The Marlinton Ranger District office (799-4334) for the Monongahela National Forest is located off of Rt. 39 East, on Cemetery Road.

HISTORICAL: Besides the depot building and adjoining office building, railroad structures remaining are the second water tank (presently being restored), water column, and concrete pump house at the north end of town. Adjacent to the tank is a concrete circle that marks the location of the turntable. The location of the coaling tipple can be seen on the trail as it leaves Marlinton on the north.

AREA ATTRACTIONS: From Marlinton north on Rt. 219 there is access to the Williams River section of the Monongahela National Forest, which has camping and trails available, the Edray State Fish Hatchery, the northern end of the Highland Scenic Highway, and Snowshoe Mountain Resort. Snowshoe (572-1000) was originally developed for skiing but now is a four season area and features a system of trails for hiking and mountain biking, as well as a golf course and other recreational opportunities. The Pocahontas County Historical Society's museum and a golf course are located on Rt. 219 South.

Marlinton and Camden Railroad Junction: Milepost 56.95 (south switch).

A 1,530 foot siding on the west side of the main track, connected on both ends, served as the interchange track between the Marlinton and Camden Railroad and the Greenbrier Division. The M&C was the logging railroad of the Campbell Lumber Company (1905–1914) which had its mill at Campbelltown. The siding was removed in early 1915.

HISTORICAL: The piers of the lumber company bridge can be seen in the river.

FIFTY-SEVEN: Milepost 57.44 (switch).

Location of the sawmill of the Greenbrier River Lumber Company (1900–1904), to the west of the track. The spur serving the mill was connected on the north end. The spur was gone by 1916 but was probably removed in 1906 when the station was removed from the station list.

As a named station, Fifty-seven did not appear on the station list until October 1902. It was no longer on the April 1906 list.

This photograph fits the description of a wreck at Milepost 59 on September 26, 1910. The fireman suffered minor injuries while the engineer escaped without injury. PCHS

Siding: Milepost 58.70.

A stub siding 281 feet long was installed at this location in 1927 for the Marlin Lumber Company. In July 1928 it was moved to Milepost 51.47. It was on the east side of the main line and connected on the south end.

SIXTY: Milepost 59.34 (switch).

A stub siding about 570 feet in length was located here on the east side of the main track and connected on the south end. It was installed in 1906 for the sawmill of the Graham-Yeager Lumber Company (later Brown, Depp and Swanson) (1906–c. 1911). The station was briefly referred to as YEAGER.

The station was first on the January 1907 station list and no longer on the April 1914 list. The siding was removed in 1913.

KNAPP: Milepost 59.36.

In 1920 a 350-foot stub siding was constructed for the Marlinton Wood Company (1920–?) on the site of the earlier siding (above).

The siding was removed in 1928 and Knapp was no longer on the station list in September 1930. It first was listed on the July 1921 station list.

Forest Service Road 300A: Milepost 59.45. Take this road up Marlin Mountain and then right on Road 300 for a 5.6 mile loop that ends at the Marlinton ranger station. Only those with experience should take this trip on a bicycle.

Halfway Run bridge: Milepost 59.46.

Siding: Milepost 59.56.

Site of a 150-foot siding installed in 1917 for the Kendall Lumber Company. It was on the east side of the main track and connected on the north end. The siding is believed to have been removed the same year as built.

AUGUST: Milepost 60.25.

Location of a spur track, connected on the north

View of the mill and logging railroad bridge at August. The C&O (trail) is in the background of the photo. B.F. KLINE

end, that served a lumber operation on Brushy Lick Run, across the river from the railroad.

At first the mill was across the river but was later on the railroad side. The operation was started in 1900 by August Brothers and finished about 1910 after going through several changes of ownership.

The spur was removed by late 1913 (probably in 1911). August was first on the October 1901 station list and was closed between the September 1930 and September 1934 lists.

Thorny Creek bridges: Mileposts 60.81 and 60.90.

THORNY CREEK: Milepost 61.28 (originally 61.02).

A 15×24 foot building described as a freight house for the Kendall Lumber Company was located here. A passenger shelter was also provided.

Thorny Creek first appeared on the January 1903 station list and was the site of a 384-foot stub siding, east of the main track and connected on the north end. This siding was gone before 1916. In 1914 the Kendall Lumber Company built a logging railroad on Thorny Creek from a junction with the C&O at this station. This line was removed in 1917. By the summer of 1923 (perhaps by 1919) a stub siding had been constructed on the site of the earlier one. It was 364 feet long, connected on the north end and removed in October 1963.

ACCESS: To access the trail at Thorny Creek, take Thorny Creek Mountain Road (Co. Rt. 11/2) from WV Rt 28 at Dilleys Mill, 4.8 miles to a small parking area. The road is unpaved, narrow, and not suitable for all drivers/vehicles.

HISTORICAL: The road joining the trail just north of the MP 61 marker was originally the logging railroad.

CLAWSON (HARPER): Milepost 62.40 (originally 62.11).

A shelter shed was provided for passengers. Other facilities here included a section foreman's house, bunk house, and section tool house.

The station appeared on the July 1901 station list as Harper but the name was given as Clawson one year later. EDRAY was briefly considered as a name for this station but never used as far as can be determined.

A 1,500-foot passing siding was located at Clawson on the west side of the main track. It was removed in early 1977.

Clawson was taken off of the freight station list in November 1956 but remained a passenger flagstop.

The name Harper is from the right-of-way grantor and Clawson is from the Rev. Samuel Clawson.

Double Culvert Hollow: Milepost 63.75 (switch).

Location of a stub siding, about 1,100 feet long, east of the main track and connected on the north end. It was installed for the Kendall Lumber Company. The siding crossed the stream and south of the creek a logging railroad spur switched from it.

C&O maintenance crew and their handcar at Clawson. PCHS

The siding was built in 1917 and removed by the middle of 1921.

Campsite: Milepost 63.77, with well and toilet.

HARTER: Milepost 64.55.

A station building, 10.5×20.5 feet, was provided here; probably of the passenger shelter/freight room layout.

The station appeared on the July 1903 station list with the beginning of operations by the Harter Brothers Lumber Company (1903–1912). A spur track served the mill (on the west side of the trail) and was probably removed in 1914; it was gone by 1916.

Harter was taken from the list of freight stations in November 1956 but continued as a flagstop for passengers.

Spur: Milepost 65.09.

Switch for a logging spur installed in 1918 for the Kendall Lumber Company. It was east of the main track and connected on the south end. The spur may have also been used by the A. D. Neill Lumber Company.

Removal date is not known.

Greenbrier River bridge: Milepost 65.24.

The track was laid across a temporary bridge here in early November 1900. The permanent bridge was put in place the next month.

HISTORICAL: The original bridge is the existing one and it is the only major bridge that was not replaced in the 1929 upgrading of the line. Only the south "tell tale" (to warn brakemen on the top of a freight car of the approaching tunnel) for the tunnel exists today.

Sharps Tunnel: Milepost 65.28 (south portal). The tunnel is 511 feet long.

Work began on the tunnel in the middle of September 1899. The name comes from members of the Sharp Family who granted right-of-way in the area.

Sawmill and town of the Harter Brothers Lumber Company. PCHS

SHARPS TUNNEL: Milepost 65.86 (switch).

Site of a 220-foot stub siding, connected on the south end and west of the main track.

This station was on the station lists for about a year, appearing on the April 1904 list and gone from the July 1905 list. It is assumed the siding was removed in 1905; it was gone by 1916.

BIG RUN: Milepost 66.73 (Originally 66.74)

This station appeared on the station list for November 1909 and was the site of a small sawmill operated by W. W. Dempsey (1909–?). To serve the mill a 700-foot stub siding was constructed on the west side of the main track. It was connected on the south end and was abandoned by 1916.

In 1912 a stub siding was constructed on the opposite side of the main track under a contract with H. E. Nixon. It was over 500 feet long and also connected on the south end. By 1916 the spur had been reduced in length to about 260 feet and removed completely by 1919.

In 1920 a stub siding was built under contract with Pasquale Anastacio on the location of the Dempsey

Early Greenbrier Division passenger train passing through Sharps Tunnel and crossing the river. The train is coming south, en route to Ronceverte. PCHS

siding. It was 465 feet long and connected on the south end. In 1922 the siding was extended 55 feet on behalf of the Williams and Pifer Lumber Company. This siding was removed in October 1963.

Big Run was removed from the freight station list in November 1956 but remained a passenger flag stop.

Big Run bridge: Milepost 67.04. Small waterfall and pool in the stream. Picnic shelter.

LOMBARDY

This station was on the station list for almost four years. It was first listed in October 1904 and gone in July 1908. Exact location is unknown at this time but it had station number 68, which implies it was near Milepost

68. A siding is indicated on station lists but no details have been found. The name may come from Italian families that lived in the area.

The curve between MP 67 and MP 68 was one of the sharpest on the Greenbrier line. Also, a train made a 180-degree change in direction going through this curve.

Campsites: Mileposts 69.53, 69.59, and 69.64, with well and toilet. The upper site is for horse groups and has horse rails.

CAMPER: Milepost 70.11 (switch).

Location of a siding put in for the Campbell-Cooper Lumber Company in 1911. It was on the west side of the main line, connected on the south end and 456 feet long. The siding was removed in early 1913.

Camper appeared on the July 1911 station list and was gone from the September 1913 list.

NICHOLS

This station appeared on the October 1901 edition of the station list with station number 70 (as did Camper) but the exact location is not known. It was no longer listed on the July 1904 list. According to station lists there was a siding but no details have been found.

HISTORICAL: In the area of MP 70 the grade for the logging railroad that ran south from Clover Lick can be seen across the river. Note the stones laid up to support the track.

CLOVER LICK: Milepost 71.17, elevation 2292.

Agency station and telegraph office with call KC. The depot building here was south of the road crossing and west of the track. As built it was about 40 feet long. By 1907, however, the freight room was lengthened and the building became 65.5 feet long (16.5 feet wide). A second freight door was added. The next change in the Clover Lick building was a reduction in size, a dubious distinc-

View of Clover Lick, looking to the south, about 1911. Smoke and
steam shot up from a locomotive as it pulled away from the depot
with a passenger train. PCHS

tion that only this depot on the Greenbrier received. In
October 1940 the freight room was removed, reducing the
length of the depot to 29 feet. The waiting room was
converted into a freight room with a freight door on each
side and the office became an office/waiting room. In
March 1932 the telegraph office was closed and the agency
at Clover Lick was changed to a commission basis. The
agency was discontinued in 1952. After the station was
closed the depot building was moved to a field not far from
the railroad. In October 1995 the structure was moved to
its present location along the trail, on the opposite side of
the road crossing from its original position.

Other facilities here included a water tank, section
foreman's house, two bunk houses, section tool house,
and stock pens.

Clover Lick was an early settlement in Pocahontas
County and the name is from the clover plant and
animal salt licks found nearby. LIGON was briefly consid-

ered by the railroad as the name for this station but never used.

The passing siding was about 1,400 feet long when first constructed in 1901 and was extended on the south end to 1,798 feet in length by 1916. It was removed in early 1977.

The track arrangement on the west side of the main track varied over the years. A stave mill was located at Clover Lick in 1901 by the National Cooperage Company and a spur track to it switched off from the main track, connected on the north end. By 1908 the track layout had been altered, perhaps at the time the DeRan Lumber Company (1906–1911) built its mill on Clover Creek in 1906. The spur to the now out of business stave mill was gone and an 881 foot stub siding installed. It switched from the main track just north of the depot. A spur to the DeRan mill switched from this siding. By 1910 the siding had been altered. The switch was moved to just south of the bridge over Clover Creek and the siding lengthened to 949 feet, ending behind the depot. The spur to the DeRan mill still switched from the siding. In November 1936 the depot siding was reduced in length on the south end, to 755 feet. It was removed in the summer of 1967.

A sawmill was built across the river from Clover Lick by F. S. Wise and Sons in 1913 and a 2,910-foot spur line built to it. This spur switched from the passing siding near the depot. After being sold to A. D. Neill and then to the Raine Lumber Company, the mill finally closed in 1929. The date the mill spur was removed has not been determined. Clover Lick was discontinued as a station in 1974.

ACCESS: Clover Lick is located on Back Mountain Road (Co. Rt. 1). Coming south on US Rt. 219 turn onto Rt. 1 at Edray, and then 10.6 miles to Clover Lick.

From Marlinton, take Airport Road (Co. Rt. 15) 5.2 miles to Rt. 1, then right 7.4 miles. The trail at Clover Lick is 7.0 miles south of the Rt. 66 intersection near Cass.

From WV Rt. 28 take Laurel Run Road (Co. Rt. 1/4), 2.5 miles south of Dunmore, then 4.2 miles to the trail.

FACILITIES: Parking is available between the trail and the river bridge. River access at this point also. Camping, rustic cabins, a small lake, and hiking trails are available at Seneca State Forest (800 CALL-WVA, local phone 799-6213). To reach the forest, take Laurel Run Road, then right on Rt. 28. The camping area is 5.9 miles from the trail.

HISTORICAL: The original site of the depot, south of the road crossing, is marked by a concrete foundation for a signal. Also remaining in the same area are the section house, concrete pump house, foundations for the second water tank, and piers for the lumber company bridge. Seneca State Forest was developed by the CCC program.

Clover Creek bridge: Milepost 71.38.

Present bridge was installed in 1929.

COYNER, KRYDER, ORWIG, BOCK

These stations were located between Clover Lick and Stony Bottom with exact locations now unknown. Coyner had station number 72 and was listed from October 1901 to October 1903. Kryder was number 73 and on the station lists from April 1902 to July 1903. Orwig had number 73½ and appeared on the station list in January 1903. It became number 74 with the next list, April 1903, and was no longer listed in July 1904. Bock was on the lists from October 1901 to April 1903, and had station number 74.

These stations would have been associated with timber purchases in the area by Coyner Brothers, Orwig and Kryder, and M. P. Bock.

There was a short stub siding just north of the bridge over Clover Creek, west of the main track and connected on the north end. Perhaps it was the site of the Coyner station and a mill operated by Coyner Brothers. A 150-foot siding may have been located at about milepost 73.6, west of the main track and connected on the south end. Perhaps it was Bock.

Elk Creek bridge: Milepost 74.28.

STONY BOTTOM: Milepost 74.37.

An 11×30 foot building described as a freight house was located here.

Two sidings were located at Stony Bottom to serve small sawmills on the west side of the track. A spur to the Stony Bottom Lumber Company's mill (1906–?) left the main track south of Elk Creek. It was removed in 1912.

The other siding was north of the creek and built in 1902 to serve the mill of the Buena Vista Hardwood Company (1901–mid 1920s). Connected on the south end, it was 418 feet long. In 1905 the siding was extended in length to 601 feet to also serve J. C. Haupt. In 1933 it was reduced in length to 500 feet. The siding was removed in December 1966.

The track was laid to Stony Bottom by late November 1900.

ACCESS: Stony Bottom is on Co. Rt. 1, 3.8 miles north of Clover Lick and 3.2 miles south of the Rt. 66 intersection near Cass.

FACILITIES: Lodging at a small motel in Stony Bottom.

Woods Run bridge: Milepost 74.55.

SITLINGTON (FORREST): Milepost 76.79 (second depot), elevation 2,364.

Agency station and telegraph office with call FT (changed to SG in 1906). The first depot building here was 16.5×61 feet. It was located on the west side of the track

The second depot building at Sitlington, constructed after the first depot burned in 1908, was of a different style than the original stations. Photo taken on July 29, 1911. PCHS

and north of the road crossing. This building burned on October 29, 1908. The replacement depot, 16.5×32.5 feet, was of a different style from the original Greenbrier depots as can been seen from the photo. The new depot was on the east side of the track and south of the road crossing. The agency/telegraph office was closed in September 1928. The depot building was removed in July 1947 and replaced with a 10.5×21 foot passenger shelter/freight room structure.

Other facilities at Sitlington included a water tank, section foreman's house, station agent's house, three bunk houses, another dwelling, and section tool house.

A passing siding, 2,467 feet in length, was here, on the west side of the main track rather than the more usual east side. It was removed in late 1936.

The change of name from Forrest to Sitlington was

made on May 1, 1904. The first name was from Forrest Moore and the second from a pioneer family in the area.

ACCESS: Sitlington is 3.2 miles from WV Rt. 28 at Dunmore on Sitlington Road (Co. Rt. 12). Rt. 12 continues on to Co. Rt. 1, 2.8 miles, but is unpaved, narrow, and steep.

FACILITIES: Gas, groceries, and public phone are available at Dunmore. The Allegheny Trail is part of the Greenbrier River Trail between Sitlington and Cass.

HISTORICAL: The location of the second depot is indicated by a concrete retaining wall on the east side of the trail. The shelter/freight room structure has been moved a short distance to the west on Rt. 12.

Track remaining in place, 1978–1992: Milepost 78.00. From this point to Durbin the track was purchased by the State of West Virginia after the Greenbrier Branch was abandoned in 1978.

MOSES RUN: Milepost 78.02 (switch).

Location of a small sawmill operation started by Mohn and Braucher in 1901. Before closing about 1909 it had several other owners.

A stub siding served the mill. It was about 120 feet in length, connected on the south end and west of the main track. The station was no longer on the station list with the July 1909 edition and the siding was probably removed at that time. It first appeared on the October 1901 list.

Moses Run bridge: Milepost 78.04.

RAYWOOD: Milepost 78.46, elevation 2,392.

Agency station and telegraph office with call RW. This was the only agency station established after the early years of the Greenbrier Division. It was on the station list first in September 1914. The depot served the mill and town of the Warn Lumber Corporation (later Forest

Freight train en route to Durbin nearing the Raywood station. Photo taken in the 1926–29 period by Glen Friel.

Lumber Company) (1914–1928). A 16.5×50-foot freight and passenger station was built here in 1915 on the east side of the tracks, north of the lumber company bridge. The agency/telegraph office was closed in July 1929 but the building was not removed until October 1957.

A passing siding 1,579 feet in length was installed here in the spring of 1914. The spur track to the mill and town, which were across the river from the railroad, switched from the passing track. The passing siding was removed in late 1936.

Raywood was removed from the freight station list in November 1956 but remained as a flag stop for the passenger train. The name is from the Ray Family that owned land in the area.

HISTORICAL: Piers for the Warn Lumber Corporation railroad bridge are still in place.

Campsite: Milepost 78.62, with horse rail.

Track remaining in place, 1992–2002: Milepost 79.41. In late 1992 the track was removed to this point as part of the project to repair the 1985 flood damage.

DEER CREEK: Milepost 79.55.

The store of the Range Lumber Company was located at the platform and no doubt served as a depot.

Deer Creek appeared on the station list in November 1909 with the construction of a sawmill by the Deer Creek Lumber Company (later Range Lumber Company) (1909–1922). Under a contract between the lumber company and the railroad, the C&O furnished the superstructure of the bridge the lumber company needed to cross the river to gain access to its timber. The spur to the mill on the east side was connected on the south end. It was removed in 1925.

Also located at Deer Creek was an extract plant owned by the West Virginia Pulp and Paper Company (1915–1928). This plant was served by a 2,326.5 foot siding, east of the main track, that was connected at both ends. A number of sidings switched from this track to the plant area. By 1937 this siding had been reduced to a stub siding 1305 feet long, connected on the south end. It was removed in 1943.

View, looking north, of the Range Lumber Company mill at Deer Creek. PCHS

Extract plant at Deer Creek, operated by the W. Va. Pulp and Paper Company. This facility took waste bark to produce dyes and various tannins used in tanning. WESTVACO CORP.

Deer Creek was closed between the September 1930 and September 1934 station lists.

HISTORICAL: Foundations for the extract plant are visible on the east side of the trail.

GALFORD, RISH

These two stations both had the same station number, 80. Galford was on the station list for two and a half years, January 1903–July 1905, and Rish appeared for slightly over a year, August 1909–January 1911.

At milepost 79.65 there was a switch for a 200-foot stub siding, west of the main track and connected on the south end, that was probably the location of both these stations. This siding was removed by 1916. Galford is from right-of-way grantors and Rish probably comes from J. K. Reish, who made timber purchases in the area and may have had a sawmill.

Northern Trail Head: Milepost 80.06

ACCESS: The trail head parking lot is on Deer Creek

Road (Co. Rt. 1/13), a short distance from WV Rt. 66. Deer Creek Road in 0.5 mile from the Cass Scenic Railroad depot.

FACILITIES: Information on page 80.

Track remaining in place: Milepost 80.11. From this point to Durbin the track is still on the right-of-way.

Cold Run bridge: Milepost 80.13.

Wye Track: Milepost 80.21 (south switch).

A wye track for turning locomotives was located north of Cold Run. It was removed in June 1934.

CASS: Milepost 80.68 (original depot), elevation 2,446.

Agency station and telegraph office with call CS. The original depot measured 16.5×78 feet and was located on the site of the parking lot for the present depot. In the summer of 1923 a larger depot was constructed, a few feet to the north. The new building was 20.5×92.5 feet with waiting room, 20 feet, office, 15 feet, waiting room, 15 feet, and freight room, 40 feet. A modified form of the standard style, it lacked a peaked roof over the agent's

View of Cass on February 15, 1901. That the track has been completed to this location for less than two months is obvious from its condition in the photo. The house to the left is near the site of the depot.

View taken from almost the same location as the previous photo, but several years later. This photo shows the original station building, which was located where the parking lot for the Cass Scenic Railroad depot is today. PCHS

bay window and had less gingerbread at the gables. The agency/telegraph office at Cass was closed in 1965 but the station continued to be used by the Cass Scenic Railroad. The building was destroyed by fire on May 5, 1975. The State Park System built a new depot based on the 1923 structure but with a peaked roof over the bay window. The new depot was completed in the spring of 1979.

Other facilities at Cass included a water tank, coaling platform, ash pit, section foreman's house, bunk house, motor car house, and section tool houses.

Given the size of the Cass lumber operation and the number of years it was in existence, 1900 to 1960, it is not surprising that there was a variation in the track arrangement at Cass over the years. Prior to the opening of the sawmill in January 1902 a long siding switched from the main track south of the depot and eventually became the logging railroad up Leatherbark Creek. From this track a loading siding ran in behind the depot from the north. To complete the track layout in 1901, a siding which could have served as a passing track was located east of the main track with a spur to the site of the mill construction.

With the completion of the mill the amount of track in the Cass yard expanded rapidly, coming to over 14,000 feet of track (not counting the main line). The track west of the main track became the passing siding and was 2,170 feet long in 1916. Extending from it northward was a 840-foot stub siding serving as an interchange track for

In the early morning fog on August 14, 1969, the Greenbrier local freight paused at the Cass depot on its way from Durbin. The building in this photo is the second Cass depot, which burned in 1975. PHOTO TAKEN BY PHILIP BAGDON

the cars of pulp wood for Covington. By the early teens the interchange track was not sufficient due to the increasing business and the addition of the cars of bark going to the extract plant. To provide space for more cars the interchange track was extended in 1915 to 2,530 feet and a switch added at the north end. The passing track was later shortened on the south end and became 1,930 feet in length. The track east of the main line became the major siding serving the mill complex, varying in length over the years, but in excess of 2,200 feet. The line of the logging railroad (the Greenbrier, Cheat and Elk Railroad after 1910) joined the interchange siding. Various crossover tracks, loading sidings near the depot and in the lumber yard, and a track to the mill pond completed the complex. The lumber company had its shops and engine facilities on Leatherbark Creek.

The track was completed to Cass by Christmas of 1900 and shipment of pulp wood to the paper mill at Covington, Virginia, began on January 28, 1901. Passenger service was extended to Cass on June 1, 1901. The sawmill of the W. Va. Pulp and Paper Company began production in January 1902. The Cass operation was sold to the Mower Lumber Company in 1942. It was closed in June 1960. Cass was named for Joseph Cass, a WVP&P Company official.

ACCESS: Cass is on WV Rt. 66, 11 miles from US Rt. 219 on the west and 4.5 miles from WV Rt. 28/92 on the east.

FACILITIES: Lodging and a restaurant (summer only) are available at the Cass Scenic Railroad State Park. Lodging, food, gas, groceries, banks, ATMs, and medical clinics are available at the Snowshoe Mountain Resort, to the west on WV Rt. 66, and in the Green Bank/ Arbovale area on WV Rt. 28/92. Private campgrounds are located near Cass on the Gum Road (Co. Rt. 1/2) and WV Rt. 28/92.

HISTORICAL: The Cass Scenic Railroad, which goes from Cass to Bald Knob, is the remaining section of the once extensive logging railroad system that served the Cass mill. One CSRR engine, No. 5, was constructed in 1905 and came new to Cass. It is one of the oldest operating steam locomotives in the country. The town of Cass is a well preserved "company town," typical of the lumber industry and has been designated a National Historic District. The cabins rented by the park are former lumber company employee houses. Today's Cass Country Store is located in the former lumber company store building. C&O structures remaining are the water tank (still in use by the CSRR) and section foreman's house. Left from the sawmill are the boiler house, power house, dry kilns, and mill foundation.

AREA ATTRACTIONS: The Cass Scenic Railroad (800 CALL-WV, local phone 456-4300, cassrailroad.com) offers trips to Whittaker Station and Bald Knob, the second highest point in the state at 4,842 feet. The trains are powered by steam locomotives used on logging railroads at Cass and other locations. They are operated from Memorial Day through October. The National Radio Astronomy Observatory (456-2150, gb.nrao.edu), located at Green Bank on Rt. 28/92, offers tours of its scientific facilities and educational programs at a new visitor/educational center. Its newest telescope, the Green Bank Telescope, is the largest fully steerable radio telescope in the world. Snowshoe Mountain Resort (572-1000, snowshoemtn.com) has a system of trails for hiking and mountain bikes as well as a full range of other recreational offerings. At Durbin the Durbin and Greenbrier Valley Railroad (456-4935, mountainrail.com) operates steam-powered excursion trains on five miles of the former Greenbrier Division. The West Fork Trail, the former Western Maryland Railway line along the West Fork of the Greenbrier River, begins at Durbin and extends for 22 miles. This is a Forest Service trail and information is available at the ranger office in Bartow (456-3335).

From Cass the track is still in place to Durbin, although most remains in a damaged condition due to the 1985 and 1996 floods. The future of this part of the line is uncertain. There is interest in both repairing the track for use by the Cass Scenic Railroad as well as removing it to allow the Greenbrier River Trail to be extended. Five miles have been repaired by the D&GV RR for its use. The final section of the former Greenbrier Division, from Durbin to Winterburn, has been absorbed into adjoining properties.

Stations on the Cass-Winterburn section were:

CUP RUN, MP 82.58

PINE FLATS, MP 83.31

WANLESS, MP 84.40

NIDA, MP 87.01

HOSTERMAN (COLLINS), MP 88.17, agency station and telegraph office with call CN, closed April 15, 1919

HEVNER, MP ? (Station number 90)

BOYER, MP 92.21

WHITING, MP 92.81

LENTZ, MP 93.66

DURBIN, MP 95.55, agency station and telegraph office with call DR, closed December 31, 1978.

FRANK, MP 96.48

GUM, MP 96.79

BARTOW, 97.88, agency station and telegraph office with call BR, closed in 1928.

HOUCHINS, MP 99

THORNWOOD, MP 100.46

WINTERBURN, MP 100.72, agency station and telegraph office with call WN, closed by July 1, 1920.

End of Greenbrier Division, MP 100.96.

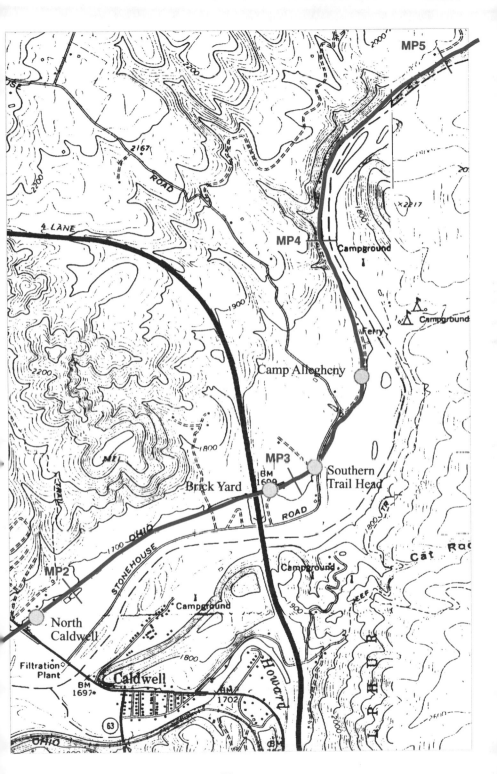

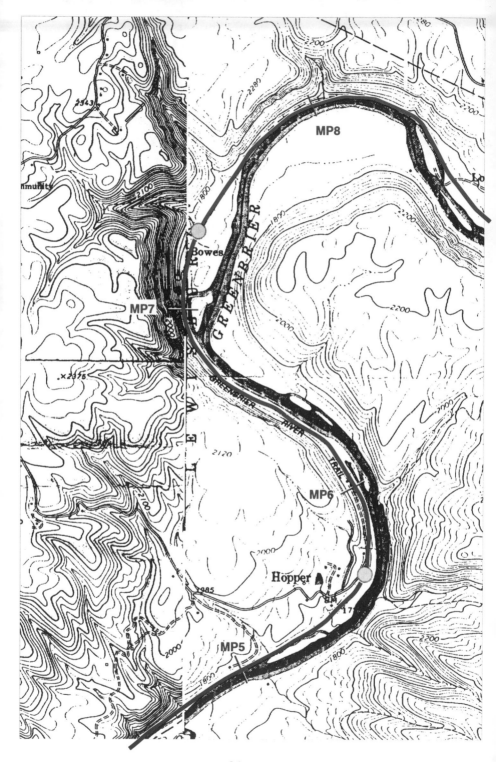

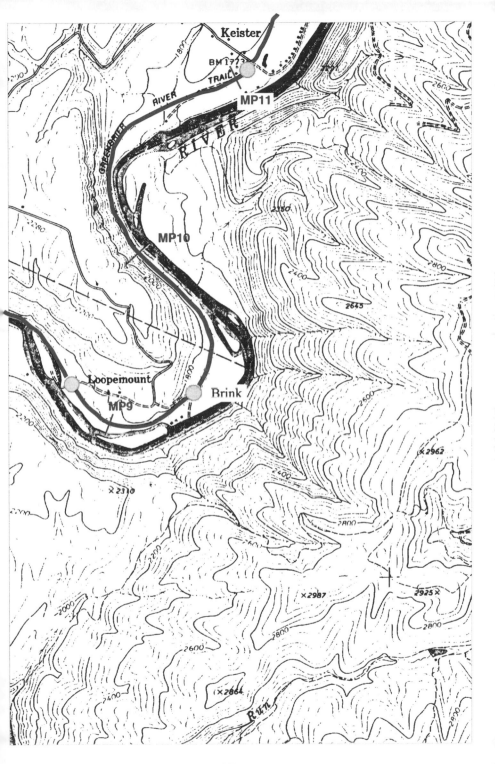

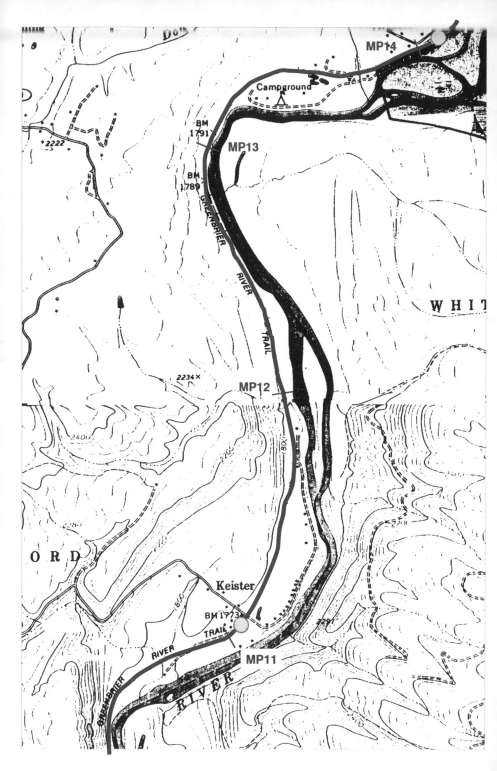

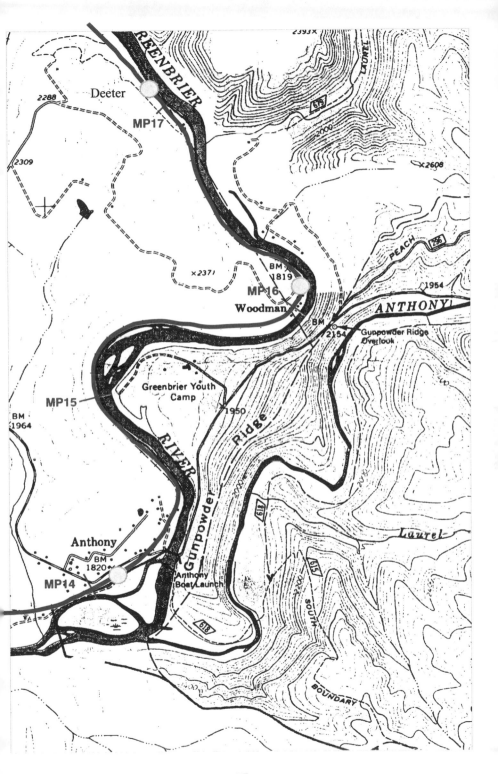

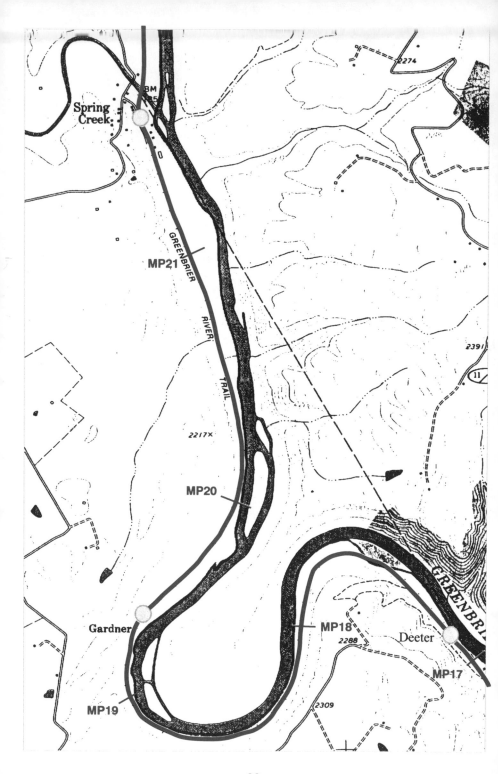

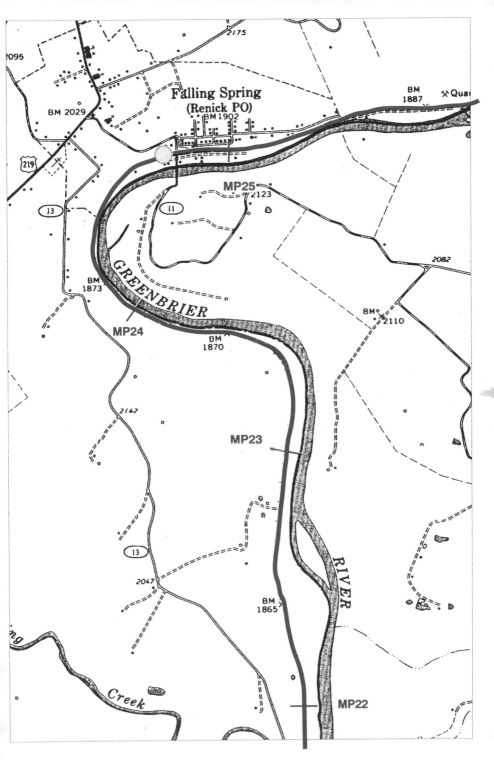

Falling Spring
(Renick PO)

BM 1902

BM 2029

2095

2175

BM
1887

Quar

219

13

11

MP25

2123

GREENBRIER

BM
1873

MP24

BM
1870

2082

BM
2110

MP23

2142

13

2047

BM
1865

RIVER

Creek

MP22

ng

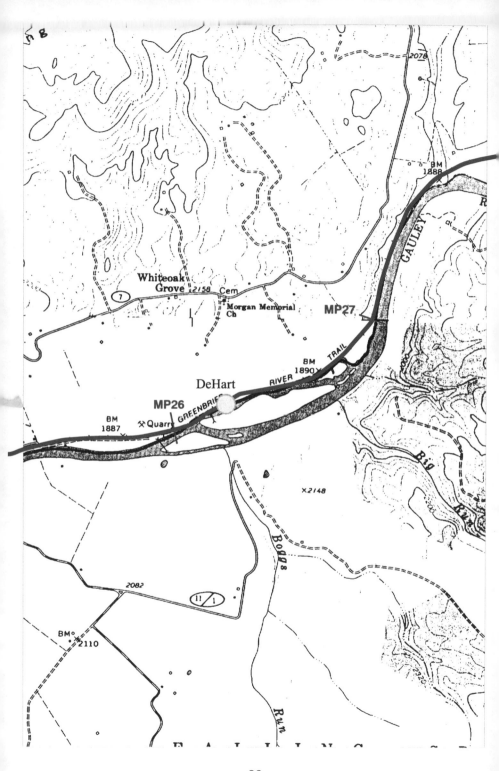

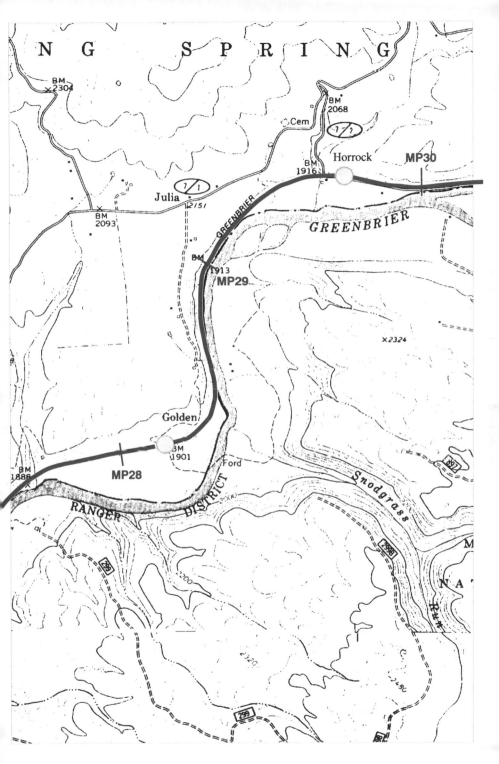

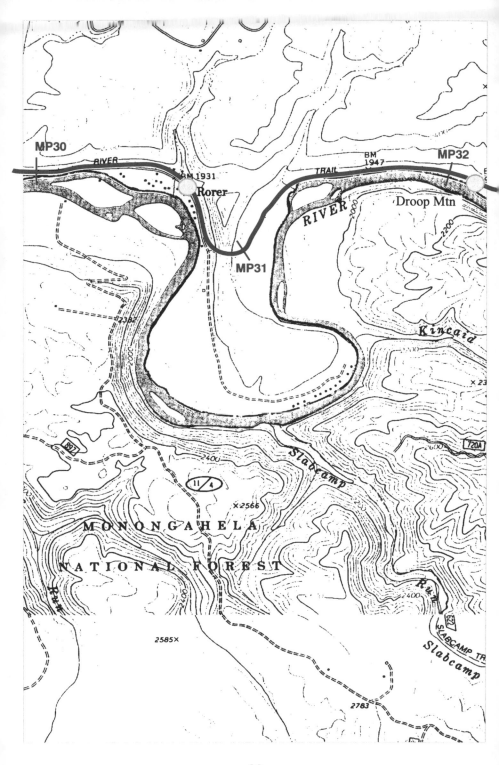

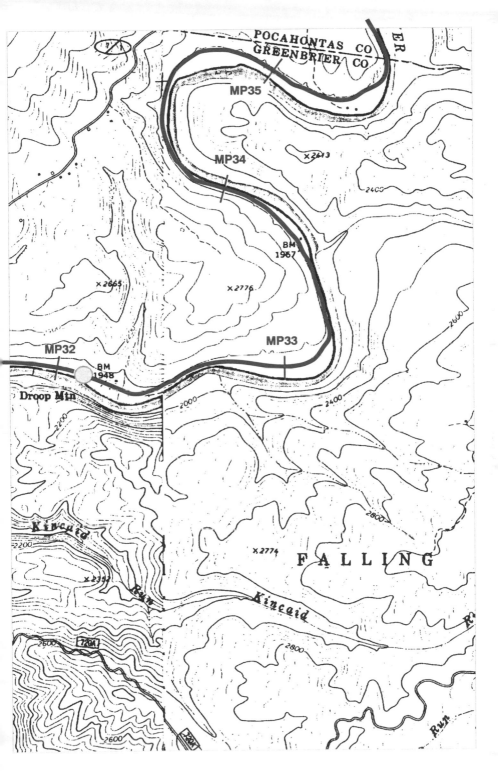

POCAHONTAS CO
GREENBRIER CO

MP35

MP34

×2613

2400

BM
1957

×2665

×2776

MP33

2600

MP32

BM
1948

Droop Mtn

2000

2400

Kincaid

2200

2800

×2774

FALLING

×2352

Run

Kincaid

R

2600

39A

2800

2600

2800

Run

93

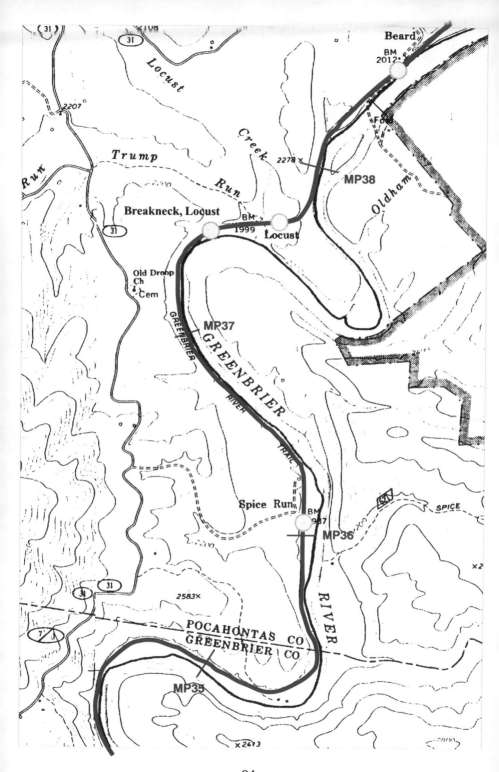

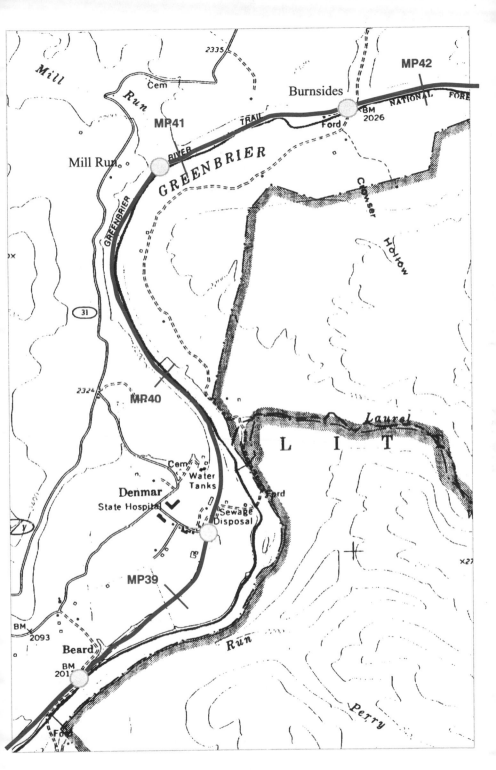

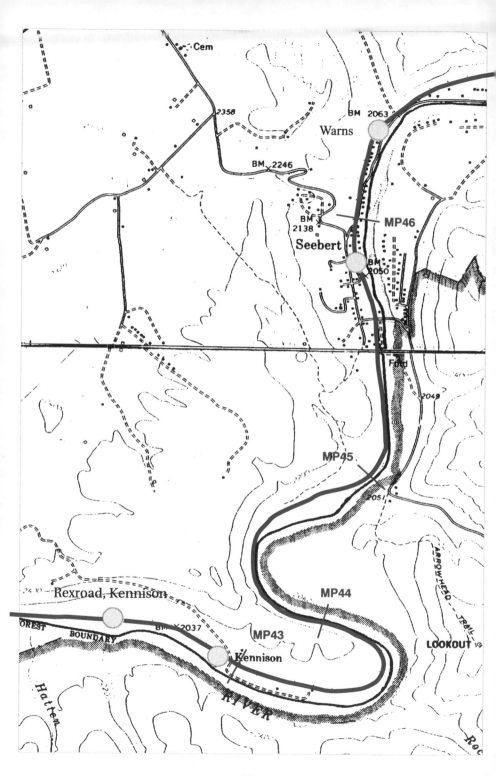

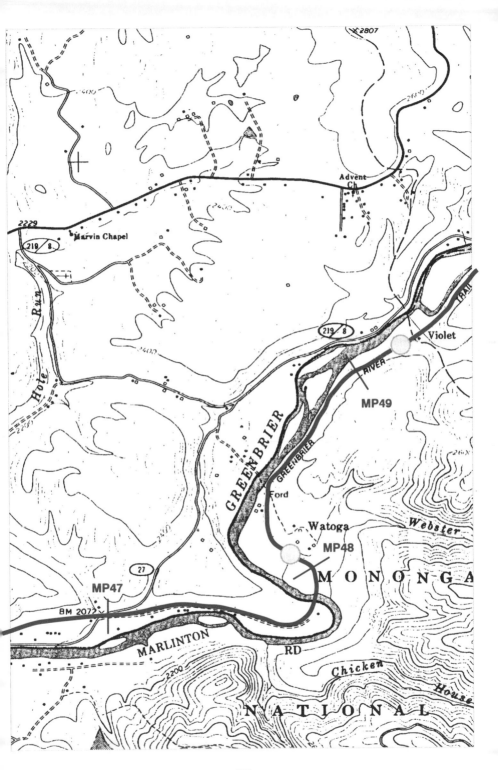

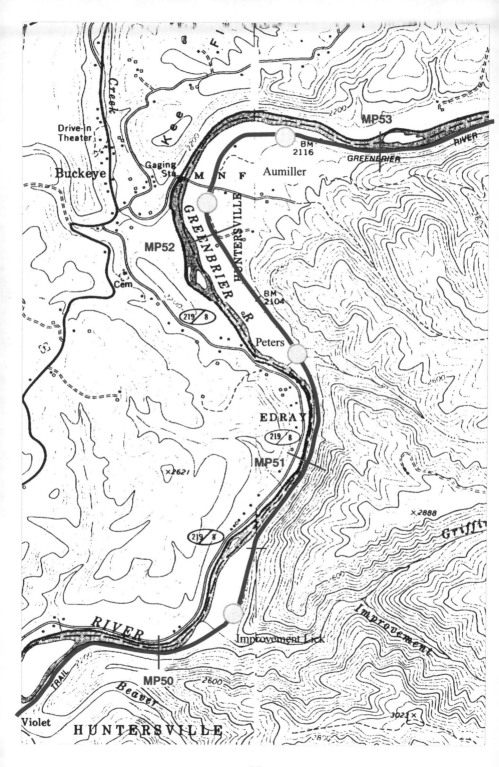

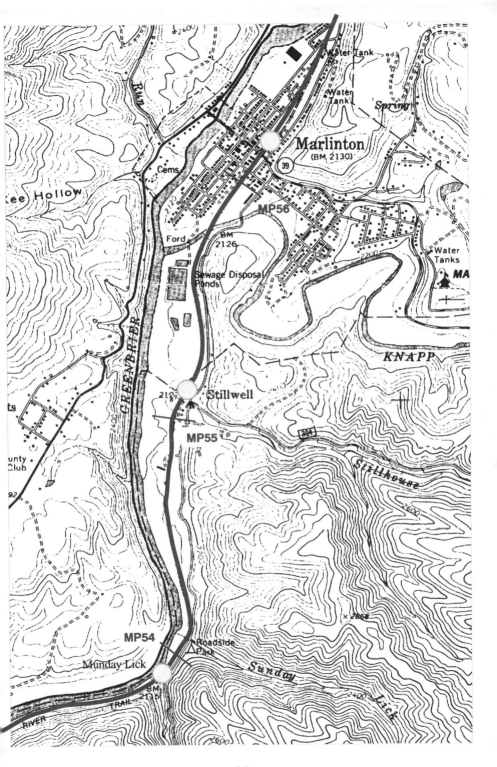

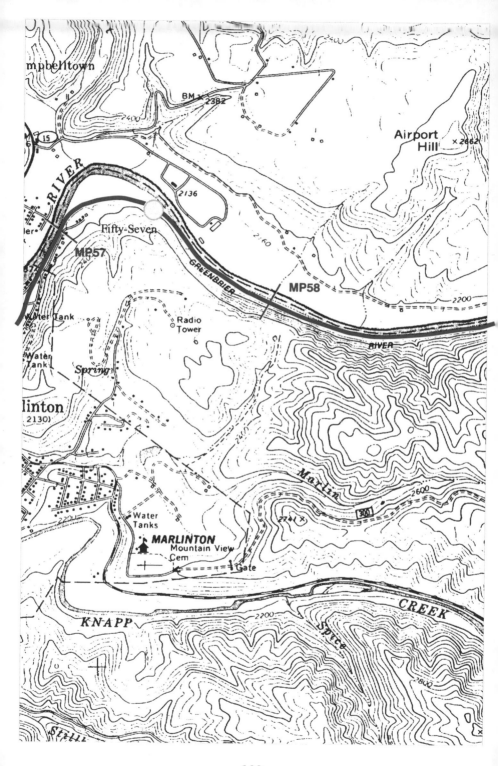

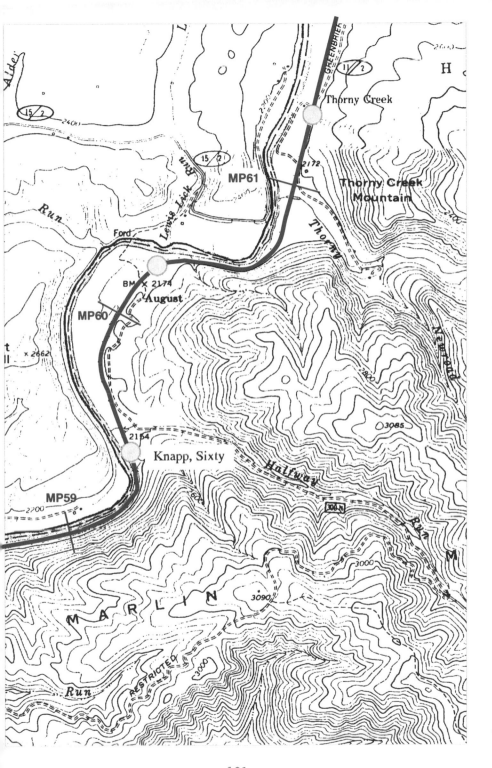

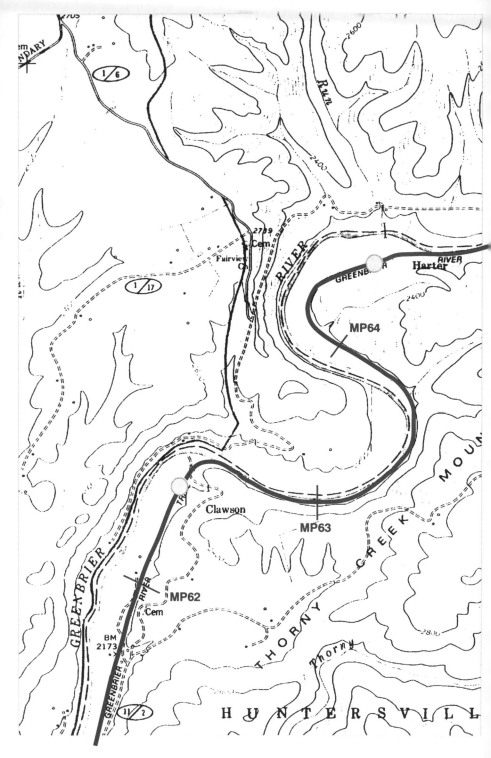

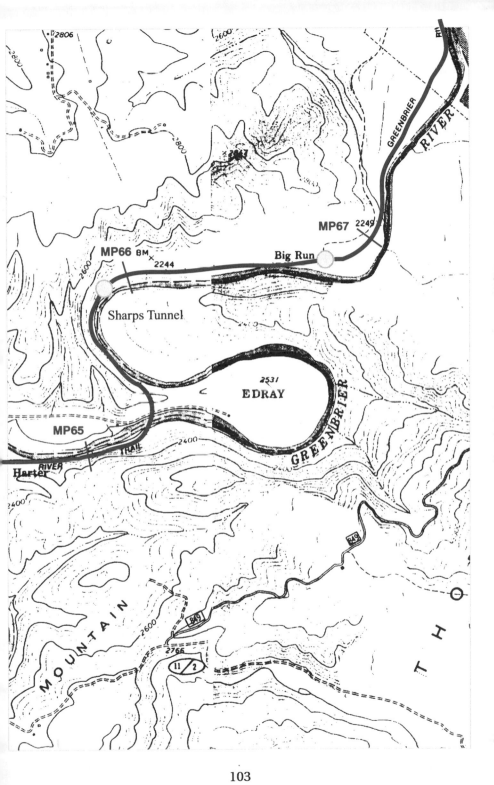

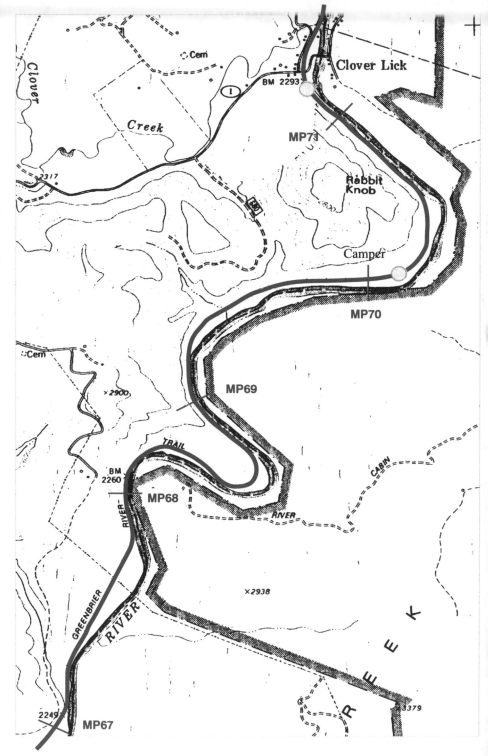

Clover Lick

BM 2293

MP73

Rabbit
Knob

Camper

MP70

MP69

TRAIL

BM
2260

MP68

RIVER

CABIN

RIVER

×2938

GREENBRIER

RIVER

C R E E K

2249

MP67

104

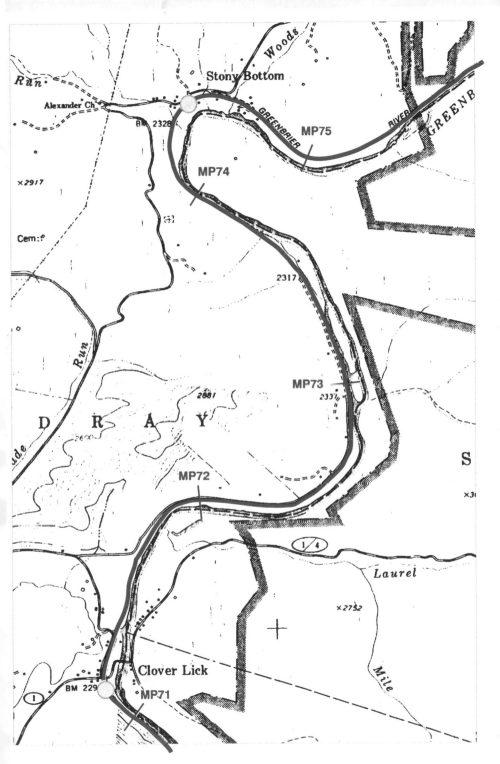

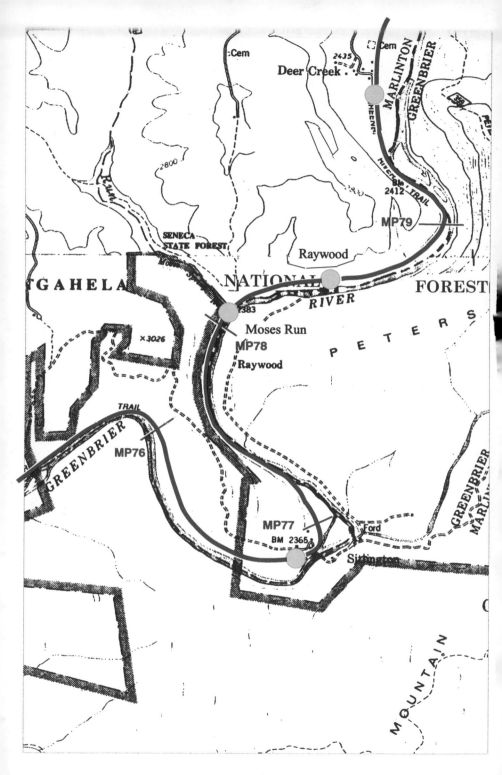

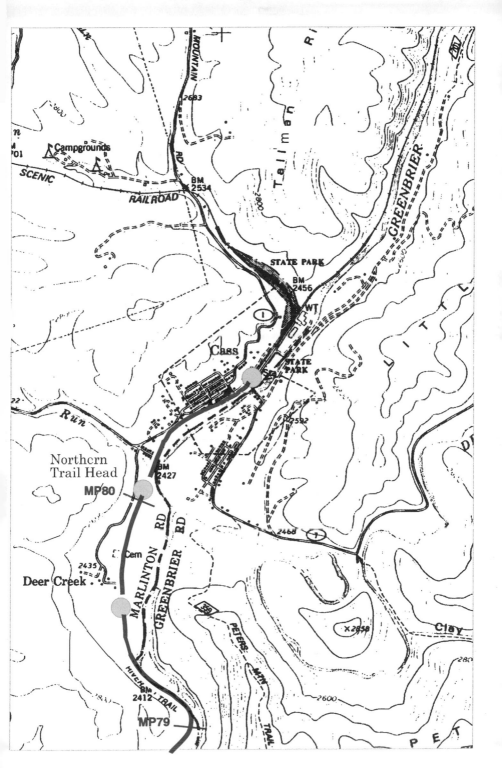

About the Author

William Price McNeel has deep roots in the Green-brier Valley of West Virginia, with his father's family in the Valley before the Revolutionary War and his mother's since the early 1800's. He grew up in Charleston, but came to his parents' home county of Pocahontas to teach school after college graduation. Following a number of years of teaching, he began working for *The Pocahontas Times*, which has been owned by the Price family since 1892. He is presently editor of the paper.

McNeel has had a lifelong interest in the history of the Greenbrier Valley area. He is the author of one book and a number of articles on the history of the area and is on the board of several local and statewide historical groups.

He has a BS degree from Marietta College and his MS from the University of Oregon. He and his wife, Denise, have one son, James.